A Handbook on Law of Torts

Material and Cases

A Handbook on

Law of Torts

Material and Cases

By

Birendra Mohan Thakur

Dean of Law, B.N.M.U, Madhepura,
Secretary, B.M.T. Law College, Purnia

and

Tarun Mishra

LL.B. (Delhi University),
LL.M. (ICFAI Hyderabad), ELT Expert,
Guest Faculty, B.M.T. Law College, Purnia

B.M.T. Law College, Purnia

in association with

New Century Publications
New Delhi, India

NEW CENTURY PUBLICATIONS
4800/24, Bharat Ram Road,
Ansari Road, Daryaganj,
New Delhi - 110 002 (India)

Tel.: 011-2324 7798, 4358 7398, 6539 6605
Fax: 011-4101 7798
E-mail: indiatax@vsnl.com • info@newcenturypublications.com
www.newcenturypublications.com

Editorial office:
LG–7, Aakarshan Bhawan,
4754-57/23, Ansari Road, Daryaganj,
New Delhi – 110 002

Tel.: 011-4356 0919

First Published: **2016**

ISBN: **978-81-7708-426-9**

Disclaimer: Although every care has been taken to avoid errors or omissions, this publication is being sold on the condition and understanding that information given in this book is merely for reference and must not be taken as having authority of or binding in any way on the author, publisher and sellers who do not owe any responsibility for any damage or loss to any person, a purchaser of this publication or not, for the result of any action taken on the basis of this work. For authoritative information, please consult prescribed text books and journals.

Published by New Century Publications and printed at Salasar Imaging Systems, New Delhi.

Designs: Patch Creative Unit, New Delhi.

PRINTED IN INDIA

Dedicated to

Late Braja Mohan Thakur

(M.A., B.L., Calcutta University)

in commemoration of his 125th birth anniversary

Foreword

It is a pleasure for me to go through *A Handbook on Law of Torts* authored jointly by Birendra Mohan Thakur and Tarun Mishra.

The learned authors have admirably dealt with the question of implementation of law of torts. This *Handbook* will go a long way in the field of education related to law.

It would be worth remembering that presently the field of civil wrong is expanding day-by-day and a variety of injuries are being caused to the general public. Awareness about civil rights has paved the way for compensation and damages. In the context of emerging scenario, the present work will serve as a useful guide for students and advocates to stake claims for compensation whenever civil wrong is committed by anybody. Additionally, by including the case law, the authors have presented the whole subject in a lucid, interesting and highly readable manner.

It is a great pleasure to the University that B.M.T. Law College, Purnia—the only NAAC accredited law college in Bihar—has published this work.

I would like to congratulate the learned authors for their dedicated and sincere efforts which have resulted in the accumulation of the entire law on subject at one place on a systematic footing. I am sure this book will be of immense help to the students, legal profession, the bench and the bar.

Professor (Dr.) Binod Kumar
Vice-chancellor,
B.N.M.U., Madhepura

About the Book

Tort means a civil wrong. Tort cases include injury in road accidents, injury or death due to spurious foodstuffs, negligent treatment in hospitals, excesses by police authorities etc.

Tort is breach of some duty independent of the contract which has caused damage to the plaintiff giving rise to civil cause of action and for which remedy is available. If there is no remedy, it cannot be called a tort because the essence of tort is to give remedy to the person who has suffered injury.

In India, tort law is a relatively new area based on common law, supplemented by codifying statutes including statutes governing damages. While India generally follows the English law, there are certain differences which may indicate judicial activism, hence creating controversy.

There is little tort litigation in India due to: (a) lack of awareness about one's rights, (b) spirit of tolerance among Indians, (c) high cost of litigation which is beyond the means of poor people, (d) undue delay—particularly in civil cases—in the final disposal of cases and (e) discouraging attitude of the courts in tort cases.

The law of torts has a social relevance in India where illiteracy and ignorance are widespread. The marginalized and vulnerable sections of the society, particularly in rural areas, do not understand their rights and privileges under the Constitution of India and the laws enacted thereunder. The law of tort needs to be understood by one and all.

The present *Handbook* explains the law of tort in simple and easily comprehensible language. It will be of immense help to students and practitioners of law.

About the Authors

Birendra Mohan Thakur is presently Dean of Law, B.N.M.U. Madhepura. He is also secretary, B.M.T. Law College, Purnia (Bihar). He established the Braja Mohan Thakur Law College, Kamla Bhawan, Purnia in the year 1982. During his tenure as founder principal of the college, the college got autonomous status from the University Grants Commission (UGC), New Delhi and accreditation (Grade B) by the National Assessment and Accreditation Council (NAAC), Bangalore.

Tarun Mishra did his LL.B. from the University of Delhi, Delhi. He has done his LL.M. from the ICFAI, Hyderabad. He is presently academic adviser of the B.M.T. Law College, Purnia (Bihar). He has also been director of TMEC, Darbhanga (a government approved institution working in the field of skill development since 2000). He is also associate editor of *Ankur*—an environmental awareness journal.

Contents

Preface

The word *tort* has been derived from the Latin term *tortum*, which means to twist. It includes that conduct which is not straight or lawful, but, is twisted, crooked or unlawful. Whenever a wrongdoer violates some legal rights vested in another person, his conduct is said to be tortuous.

The law of torts was developed in England, to redress the violation of the lawful right of a person. It developed mainly as a result of judicial decisions, where the English judges recognized the creation of new torts from time to time to do substantive justice to the people.

As a general rule, the principles of English law have been deemed to be applicable in India. However, the Indian courts are not bound to follow them and they may adopt different principles if justice, equity and good conscience so demand.

There is very little legislation in the area of tort in India. The law of torts is mainly the product of judicial pronouncements. As a general rule, the principles of English law are followed in India. Tort means a civil wrong. Tort cases include injury in road accidents, injury or death due to spurious foodstuffs, negligent treatment in hospitals, excesses by police authorities etc.

There is no comprehensive and scientific definition of the term tort. The reason is that different wrongs included under this head are of diverse species. Broadly speaking, tort may be defined as a civil wrong which is redressible by an action for unliquidated damages. When the compensation is not previously determined but left to the discretion of the court, it is said to be unliquidated damage.

Tort belongs to the category of civil wrongs. The basic nature of civil wrong is different from a criminal wrong. In the case of a civil wrong, the injured party, i.e. the plaintiff (complainant) institutes civil proceedings against the wrongdoer, i.e. the defendant. In such cases, the main remedy is damages. The plaintiff is compensated by the defendant for the injury caused to him by the defendant. Thus, damages are the most important remedy for tort. After the wrong has been committed, it is the monetary compensation which may satisfy the injured party.

In the case of criminal wrong, the criminal proceedings against the accused are brought by the state. Moreover, in the case of a criminal wrong, the individual, who is the victim of a crime (say, for example, attempt to murder) is not compensated. Justice is administered by punishing the wrongdoer in such a case.

Tort is civil wrong other than a mere breach of contract. A breach of contract is also a civil wrong but it cannot be considered a tort. Thus, if a person agrees to purchase a smart phone and thereafter does not fulfil his obligation, the wrong will be a breach of contract. Thus, every tort is a civil wrong, but every civil wrong is not a tort. Breach of contract is a civil wrong but it is not a tort.

It is only by the process of elimination that we may be able to know whether the wrong is a tort or not. Firstly, we have to see whether the wrong is civil or criminal. If it is civil then secondly, does it exclusively belong to another recognized category of civil wrongs such as breach of contract? If not, it is a tort.

There is little tort litigation in India due to: (a) lack of awareness about one's rights, (b) spirit of tolerance among Indians, (c) high cost of litigation which is beyond the means of poor people, (d) undue delay—particularly in civil cases—in the final disposal of cases and (e) discouraging attitude of the courts in tort cases.

The law of torts has a social relevance in India where illiteracy and ignorance are widespread. The marginalized and vulnerable sections of the society, particularly in rural areas, do not understand their rights and privileges under the Constitution of India and the laws enacted thereunder. The law of torts needs to be understood by one and all.

The present *Handbook* explains the law of tort in simple

and easily comprehensible language. It will be of immense help to students and practitioners of law.

The authors shall be obliged if mistakes are brought to their notice for carrying out necessary corrections in the next edition.

Suggestions and correction from the readers shall be duly considered and thankfully acknowledged.

We owe gratitude to Dr. Suman Kumar, IIT, Roorkee and Mr. Anant Bharti, Research Scholar in Law for providing technical and legal support. We extend our thanks to our family members for their forbearance and moral support at every stage of the completion of this work

Purnia **Birendra Mohan Thakur**
Tarun Mishra

1

Meaning and Definitions

1.1 Meaning of Tort

The word 'tort' has been derived from the Latin term 'tortum', which means to twist. It includes that conduct which is not straight or lawful, but, is twisted, crooked or unlawful. [1] Whenever a wrongdoer violates some legal rights vested in another person, his conduct is said to be tortuous.

The law of torts was developed in England, to redress the violation of the lawful right of a person. It developed mainly as a result of judicial decisions, where the English judges recognized the creation of new torts from time to time to do substantive justice to the people.

As a general rule, the principles of English law have been deemed to be applicable in India. [2] However, the Indian courts are not bound to follow them and they may adopt different principles if 'justice, equity and good conscience' so demand. For instance, in *M.C. Mehta vs. Union of India,* AIR 1987 SC 1086, the Supreme Court held that it was not bound by the rule of 'strict liability' laid down in *Rylands vs. Fletcher,* (1868) LR 3 HL 330, in 1868. [3] It evolved the rule of 'absolute liability' in preference to the English rule of strict liability.

1.2 Definitions

Some of the definitions given by eminent jurists are as follows:

Salmond defined it as 'a civil wrong for which the remedy is a common law action for unliquidated damages and which is not exclusively the breach of a contract or the breach of a trust or other merely equitable obligation'. [4]

Winfield stated, 'tortuous liability arises from the breach of a duty primarily fixed by the law; this duty is towards persons generally and its breach is redressable by an action for unliquidated damages'. [4]

Fraser called it 'an infringement of a right *in rem* of a private individual giving a right of compensation at the suit of the injured party'. [4]

Section 2(m) of the Limitation Act, 1963: 'Tort means a civil wrong which is not exclusively a breach of contract or breach of trust'. [3]

The above definitions and provisions suggest that tort is a civil wrong in opposition to a criminal wrong, and that every civil wrong is not a tort. There are other civil wrongs as well, like the breach of contract and breach of trust. Tort as a civil wrong is exclusive of breach of contract or breach of trust.

The phrase *unliquidated damages* needs a deliberation at this point. Damages in the case of tort are always unliquidated. Liquidated damages mean such compensation which has been previously determined or agreed to by the parties. [1] When the compensation has not been so determined but the determination of the same is left to the discretion of the court, [5] the damages are said to be unliquidated. It is very clear that there is no possibility of any such pre-determination of damages in the case of tort. This is the point where we can distinguish tort from other civil wrongs like breach of trust and breach of contract where the damages may be liquidated.

In *Jayalaxmi Salt Works Pvt. Ltd. vs. State of Gujarat,* (1994)4 SCC1, the apex court observed, 'Tort' dictionarily means "breach of duty leading to damage". The same meaning attaches to it in the law. In general, tort consists of some act done without just cause or excuse. "The law of tort exists for the purpose of preventing men from hurting one another whether in respect of their property, their presence, their reputations or anything which is theirs". The non-observance of duty and thus injury or damages caused are the basic ingredients of tort. The liability in tort may be 'strict liability', 'absolute liability' or 'special use bringing with it increased danger to others' or 'fault liability'. [6] Such liability gives rise to action in torts. Since duty is the primary yardstick to determine the tortuous liability, it always depends on the fairness and practicality of the situation, etc.

The basic aspect of the law of torts is 'no one has the right to injure or harm others intentionally or even unintentionally or innocently'. [7] However, for social development, orderly growth of the society and cultural refineness, the liberal approach to tortuous liability by courts is more conducive.

In a welfare society, construction of dams or *bandh* for the sake of community is an essential function and use of land or accumulation of water for the benefit of society cannot be non-natural use. But that cannot absolve the state from its duty of being responsible to its citizens for such violations as are actionable and result in damage, loss or injury. [8] What is fundamental is injury and not the manner in which it has been caused. In the present case, the appellants suffered loss due to the action of Government officers both at the stage of construction of dams and failure to take steps even at the last moment; it was liable to be compensated. [7]

To get the clear concept of tort it needs to be distinguished from crime, breach of contract and breach of trust.

1.3 Distinction between Tort and Crime

1. **Tort**: It is a private wrong that means an infringement of the private or civil rights of an individual. It is comparatively less serious and labeled as civil wrong. For example, an obstruction outside a particular house is a tort.
   Crime: It is a public wrong that means a wrong against the State, even though the victim is an individual. It is a more serious wrong. For example, an obstruction in the middle of a public road is a crime.
2. **Tort**: The rules applicable in a case of tort are generally different from those in the case of crime. For example, in

the case of tortuous liability for the wrong of defamation, truth is in itself a defense.

Crime: In an action for the offence of defamation, the defense of truth can be taken if the publication was made for public good.

3. **Tort**: The suit has to be filed by the injured party as plaintiff and by none else. Parties may enter into a compromise and the suit may be withdrawn.

   Crime: The criminal proceedings are not brought by the injured party but by the State. Except in certain exceptional cases, the law does not permit a settlement in criminal cases.

4. **Tort:** Damages or compensation towards the injured party to make good the loss suffered by him is the most common remedy of a tort.

   Crime: The wrongdoer is punished so as to deter him and other potential offenders from committing wrongs. In certain exceptional cases e.g. Section 357 of the Code of Criminal Procedure (CrPC), provision for compensation is also provided for.

1.4 Distinction between Tort and Breach of Contract

1. **Tort**: In tort, the duties are primarily fixed by the law and a breach of these duties constitutes a tort.

   Breach of Contract: In a contract, the duties are fixed by the parties themselves, the breach of which is a breach of contract.

2. **Tort**: A tort is a violation of a right *in rem* i.e. against the world at large. [3]

   Breach of Contract: A breach of contract is the violation of the right *in personam,* i.e. against some determinate person. In other words, the duty is based on the privity of contract and each party owes duty only to the other contracting party. Thus, a stranger to contract cannot sue. [9]

3. **Tort:** In tort, motive may be taken into account, while deciding the case. If the motive was found good and a

wrong had been done to avoid a greater evil, the defaulter might escape the liability.

Breach of Contract: In breach of contract, the defaulting party is bound to incur liability irrespective of the motive. [3]

4. **Tort:** In a tort, the damages awarded are unliquidated that is not previously fixed but decided by the courts. Generally, the parties are not known to each other until the tort is committed and moreover it is difficult to visualise before hand the quantum of loss in the tort.

   Breach of Contract: In a breach of contract, the plaintiff is awarded the damage which is either already settled between the parties i.e., liqudated damages, or the actual damages which can be determined from the relevant facts.

In *Rajkot Municipal Corporation vs. Manjulben J. Naukam* (1987) 9 SCC 552, the Supreme Court observed, "In tort, liability is primarily fixed by law, while in contract, they are fixed by the parties themselves. In tort, the duty is towards the persons generally, while in contract, it is towards specific person or persons. If the claim depends upon proof of the contract, action does not lie in tort. If the claim arises, from the relationship between the parties, independent of contract, an action would lie in tort at the election of plaintiff, although he might alternatively have pleaded in contract".

1.5 Distinction between Tort and Quasi-Contract

When a person gains some advantage or benefit to which some other person was entitled to or by such advantage another person suffers an undue loss, the law may compel the former to compensate the latter in respect of advantage so gained. The law of quasi-contract covers such obligations. It signifies liability, not exclusively referable to any other head of the law, imposed upon a particular person to pay money to another person on the ground of unjust benefit. [10] For example, A, a tradesman, leaves good at B's house by mistake. B treats the goods as his own. He is bound to pay A for them.

[11] Similarly, if A and B jointly owe ₹ 100 to C, A pays the amount to C, B not knowing the fact, pays ₹ 100 again to C, C is bound to repay the amount to B. [12] The common point between a tort and a quasi-contract is that the duty in each case is imposed by the law. The main distinction between a quasi-contract and a tort is that the law of quasi-contract gives a right only with respect to money and generally it is a liquidated sum of money. Law of torts, apart from the right to damage, grants other remedies also. Another distinctive point is that in a quasi-contract, the duty is always towards a particular person, whereas under the law of torts the duty is towards persons generally.

1.6 Distinction between Tort and Breach of Trust

In as much as in the case of breach of trust by the trustee, the beneficiary can claim such compensation which depends upon the loss that the trust property has suffered. The amount of damages is, therefore, liquidated. [3] On the other hand, damages in tort are unliquidated. Besides this, law of trust is based on fiduciary relationship between the parties, while a tort can occur between the strangers.

After giving consideration to the above discussion, we can take tort in the following propositions:

- That it is one of the forms of civil wrong.
- That it is distinct from civil wrongs such as the breach of contract and the breach of trust.
- That it is the infringement of a right *in rem* (a right given by law) as opposed to the infringement of right *in personam.*
- And that it is redressable in a court of law by asking for unliquidated damages (i.e. which are not pre-determined).

2

Liability in Tort: Conditions

The conditions for liability in tort are as under:

1. An act or omission on the part of the defendant. [13]
2. Intention or negligence or breach of a strict duty on the part of the defendant. [13]
3. Damage to the plaintiff. [13]

2.1 Act or Omission

The first requirement is that there must be an act or omission. 'An act is always voluntary; mere physical movement is not enough, e.g., sleepwalker'.

2.2 Intention

Intention is a state of mind. Where a person does an act with knowledge or desire of its consequences he is said to intend those consequences. A person is also presumed to intend the necessary or natural consequence of his act.

2.2.1 Negligence: In negligence, there is no desire for consequence. There is simply carelessness or indifference. 'A careless man is one who is not sufficiently anxious that his activities shall not be the cause of loss to others'.

2.2.2 Breach of Strict Duty: In some cases, liability is independent of intention or negligence; for example, the owner is responsible for injuries caused by his cattle straying from his land to the adjoining land. Similarly, if a person brings or accumulates on his land anything which, if it should escape, may cause damage to his neighbor, he does so at his peril. If it does escape and causes damage, he is responsible, however careful he may have been and whatever precautions he may have taken to prevent damage (*Rylands vs. Fletcher*). [14]

2.3 Damages

There is no liability unless damage or loss has resulted to the plaintiff. There must be some casual connection between the wrongful act and damage sustained by the plaintiff. [15] Damage referred here means legal damages. If the plaintiff suffers damages without any legal injury, then he cannot make liable to defendant according to the rule of maxim *damnum sine injuria.*

2.3.1 *Injuria Sine Damno*: *Injuria sine damno* means violation of a legal right without causing any harm, loss or damage to the plaintiff.

2.3.2 Two Kinds of Torts: Firstly, those tort which are actionable *per se*, i.e. actionable without the proof of any damage or loss. For instance, trespass to land is actionable even though no damage has been caused as a result of the trespass. Secondly, the torts, which are actionable only on the proof of some damages caused by an act [16]. *Injuria sine damno* covers the first of the above stated cases. In such cases, there is no need to prove that as a consequence of an act the plaintiff has suffered any harm. For a successful action, the only thing which has to be proved is that the plaintiff's legal right has been violated, i.e., there is *injuria.* [16]

Ashby vs. White is a leading case explaining the maxim *injuria sine damno.* In this case, the plaintiff succeeded in his action, even though the defendant's action did not cause any damage. The plaintiff was a qualified voter at a parliamentary election, but the defendant, a returning officer, wrongfully refused to take plaintiff's vote. No loss was suffered by such refusal because the candidate for whom he wanted to vote won the election in spite of that. [17] In *Bhim Singh vs. State of J&K,* the petitioner, an MLA of the J&K Assembly, was wrongfully detained by the police while he was going to attend the Assembly session. [1] He was not produced before the magistrate within the requisite period. As a consequence of this, the member was deprived of his constitutional right to attend the Assembly session. There was also violation of fundamental right to personal liberty guaranteed under Article 21 of the Constitution. [18] By the time the petition was decided by the Supreme Court, Bhim Singh had been released, but by way of constitutional relief, exemplary damages amounting to ₹ 50,000 were awarded to him.

2.3.3 ***Damnum Sine Injuria*****:** It means damage which is not with an unauthorized interference with the plaintiff's lawful right. Causing of damage, however substantial, to another person is not actionable in law unless there is also violation of a legal right of the plaintiff. This is generally so when the exercise of legal right by one person results in consequential harm to other. [19] "The mere fact that a man is injured by another's act gives in itself no cause of action; if the act is deliberate, the party injured will have no claim in law even though the injury is intentional, so long as the other party is exercising a legal right".

Gloucester Grammar School case [20] explains the point. There, the defendant, a schoolmaster, set up a rival school to that of the plaintiffs. Because of the competition, the plaintiff had to reduce their fees from 40 pence to 12 pence per scholar per quarter. It was held that the plaintiff had no remedy for the loss thus suffered by them. Hankford J. said, "*Damnum may be abseque injuria,* as if I have a mill and my neighbour builds another mill whereby the profit of my mill diminished, I shall have no action against him, although I am damaged…but if a miller disturbs the water from going to my mill, or does any nuisance of the like sort, I shall have such action as the law gives". In *Mogul Steamship Co. vs. McGregor Gow and Co.*, a number of steamship companies combined together and drove the plaintiff company out of the tea-carrying trade by offering reduced freight. The House of Lord held that the plaintiff had no cause of action as the defendants had by lawful means acted to protect and extend their trade and increase their profits.

3

General Defences in Tort

In an action for a tort, there are some defences which may help the defendant to avoid his liability. There are some general defences which may be taken against action for a number of wrongs. [21]

3.1 *Volenti Non Fit Injuria*

As a general proposition, it may be noted that every tort has its defence. When the plaintiff brings an action against the defendant, the defendant may avoid this liability by taking the plea of some defence that is available to him. [21] One such defence is the defence of *volenti non fit injuria,* or the defence of "consent".

When a person consents to the infliction of some harm upon himself, he has no remedy for that in tort, [22] as no man can enforce a right which he has voluntarily waived or abandoned. [23] Salmond has said that such consent may be express (consent to intentional acts) or implied (taking the risk of accidental harm). Implied consent is inferred from the conduct of the parties.

To plead this defence successfully, three things should be proved concurrently:

1. That the plaintiff had knowledge of the risk.
2. That he fully appreciated the risk.
3. That he freely and voluntarily accepted the risk.

It is also necessary that the act causing the harm must not go beyond the limit of what has been consented.

Even if all the requirements are proved, the defence can still be defeated if the plaintiff can prove foul play, willful assault or negligence on the part of the defendant.

The following cases further illustrate the scope and application of the doctrine.

In *South Indian Industries Ltd. vs. Alamelu Ammal* [15] AIR 1923 Mad 565, the defendants used a method of breaking up cast iron which consisted of dropping a heavy weight from a great height. Consequently, a piece of iron hit and killed a workman. It was held that the defence of consent was not available. That the plaintiff (workman) had some knowledge of the danger is not sufficient. A man cannot voluntarily undertake a risk the extent of which he does not appreciate.

In *Illot vs. Wikes* (1820) 3 B and Ald. 304, a trespasser, who knew about the presence of spring guns on a land, could not recover damages when he was shot by a spring gun. Similarly, damage caused to a trespasser by broken glass or spikes on the wall, or a fierce dog, is not actionable.

In *Imperial Chemical Industries vs. Shatwell,* (1965) AC 656, it was held that when a workman ignores employer's instructions and contravenes statutory provisions thereby causing damage to himself, he can certainly be met with the defence of *volenti non fit injuria.*

In *T.C.Balkrishnan vs. T.R. Subramaniam,* AIR 1968 Ker 151, an explosive which normally flew perpendicularly into the sky before it exploded, burst in the midst of a crowd in a *maidan* causing injury to a spectator. It was held that the spectator did not voluntarily assume the risk. The area was open to the public and the spectator in a big crowd of lakhs could not be said to assume the risk voluntarily. Moreover there was negligence on the part of the person firing the explosive.

In *Padmavati vs. Dugganaika* (1975) 1 Karn LJ 93, two persons took lift in a jeep. Suddenly one of the bolts fixing the right front wheel to the axle gave way toppling the jeep. The two strangers were thrown out and sustained injuries, and one of them died as a consequence of the same. It was held that the defendants' were not liable firstly, because it was a case of sheer accident and, secondly the two persons had voluntarily taken lift in the jeep and as such the principle of *volenti non fit injuria* was applicable to them.

In *Hall vs. Brooklands Auto Racing Club,* (1933) 1 KB 205, the plaintiff was a spectator at a motor car race. During the race, there was a collision between two cars, one of which was thrown among the spectators, thereby injuring the plaintiff. It was held that the plaintiff impliedly took the risk of such injury, as any spectator could see that danger was inherent in the sport. The defendant was therefore held not liable.

It may be noted that 'consent' must be free. If the consent is obtained by fraud or under compulsion or under some mistaken impression, such consent does not serve as a good defence.

In *R vs. Williams* (1923) 1 KB 340, it was held that the consent obtained by fraud does not serve the good defence. In this case, a music teacher was held guilty of rape when he had sexual intercourse with a girl under pretense that his act was an operation to improve her voice.

Similarly, consent obtained under compulsion is no consent in the eyes of the law. Furthermore, mere knowledge does not necessarily imply that the plaintiff has agreed to suffer the consequences of the risky job which he has undertaken. Thus in *Bowster vs. Rowley Reigs Corporation* (1944) KB 476, the plaintiff was asked by the defendants to drive a horse which was known to bolt. The plaintiff protested but ultimately obeyed the order. The horse bolted and the plaintiff was injured thereby. It was held the maxim *volenti non fit injuria* did not apply as compulsion negated free consent and the plaintiff was entitled to recover damages.

3.2 Exception to the Defence of *Volenti Non Fit Injuria*

The scopes of the doctrine have been limited judicially in rescue cases, and by the English Parliament vide the Unfair Contract Terms Act, 1977. 'Rescue cases' refer to that genre of cases where the plaintiff voluntarily encounters a risk to rescue somebody from an imminent danger created by the wrongful act of the defendant. In such cases, the author of the original negligence is precluded from pleading the defence of *volenti non fit injuria.*

The rationale behind this doctrine has been propounded by J. Cardozo in *Waagner vs. International Railway Co.* (1921) 232 N.Y. 176, in the following words, "Danger invites rescue. The cry of distress is the summon to relief. The law does not ignore those reactions. It recognizes them as normal. The wrong that imperils life is a wrong to the rescuer also. The risk of rescue is born of the occasion for which the negligent person is responsible". In this case, a railway passenger was thrown out of a running train due to the negligence of the railway company. When the train stopped, his companion got down and went back to search for his friend and was injured in this process. He was allowed to recover damages.

The *Hayens vs. G. Harwood & Sons,* (1935) 1 KB 146 being a rescue case, the defence of *volenti non fit injuria* was not accepted and the defendants were held liable. It was also held that the rescuer may be one who is kith or kin of the imperiled person, a police officer who owes a duty of protection, or a mere stranger, who owes no duty, and the defendants cannot take the defence of consent against any of such persons.

In *Baker vs. T.E. Hopkins & Sons,* (1959) 1 WLR 966, it was held that the act of the rescuer was the natural and probable consequence of the defendant's wrongful act which the latter could have foreseen and therefore, the defence of *volenti non fit injuria* was not available.

3.3 Act of God

There may be certain situations when the defendant is entirely helpless, that is, an unexpected injury is caused to the plaintiff which could not have been foreseen and avoided in spite of reasonable care and such situations are recognized by the law. [24]

Act of God or vis major is a defence in such situations where the injury is caused by the working of natural forces like exceptionally heavy rainfall, storms, tempests, tides and volcanic eruptions. [24]

In Halsbury's Laws of England, an act of God is defined as, "...an accident due to a natural cause, directly or exclusively without human intervention and which could not have been avoided by any amount of foresight and pains and care reasonably to be expected of the person sought to be made liable for it, or who seeks to excuse himself on the ground of it".

Pollock defines it as "operation of natural forces, so unexpected, that no human foresight or skill could reasonably be expected to anticipate it. [25] Therefore, the two essentials [26] are:

1. There must be working of natural forces, and
2. The occurrence must be extraordinary and not one which could be anticipated and reasonably guarded against.

In *Manindra Nath vs. Mathurdas Chaturbhuj*, (1945) 49 CWN 827: AIR 1946 Cal 175, an action for damages was instituted by the plaintiff, for injury caused to him, by the fall, of a cinema advertising banner (made of cloth with a wooden frame). [27] The defendant contended that the fall of a banner was caused by a storm of unusual severity. [15] It was held that in Calcutta during the monsoons wind velocity from 31 to 48 miles per hour is sometimes experienced while gusts of wind from 21 to 33 miles per hour are not uncommon. Therefore, a gust of wind with a velocity of less than 27 miles per hour (which caused the fall of the banner) cannot be said to be so unexpected that no human foresight could reasonably be expected to anticipate it and cannot be regarded as vis major or an act of God. [28]

Again in *General Traders Ltd. vs. Pierce Leslye (India) Ltd.*, it was held that mere fury of the sea does not amount to an act of God, the fury should be of such unprecedented nature, that no prudent person could have imagined and provided for it. One such example is provided by the cases of *Nichols vs. Marsland* (1875) LR 10 Ex 255, [29] where the defendant created some artificial lakes on his land. Once there was an extraordinary heavy rainfall, stated to be the heaviest in the human memory, as a result of which the embankments of the lakes gave way. The rush of water washed away four bridges belonging to the plaintiff. It was held that the defendants were not liable as the loss had occurred due to an act of God. Similarly, in *Madras Railway Co. vs. Zamindar of Carvatenagaram,* (1984) 1A 364, the tanks burst due to exceptional rainfall, the heaviest in human memory, the defence of an act of God was allowed to be pleaded successfully.

However, if the rainfall is normal, or one which could be expected in a certain area, the defence of act of God fails. Thus, in *Kallulal vs. Hemchand*, AIR 1958 MP 48, [29] the wall of a building collapsed on a day when there was a rainfall of 2.66 inches. It was held that the defendant could not take the defence of act of God in this case as that much of rainfall during the rainy season was not something extraordinary but only such as ought to have been anticipated and guarded against.

3.4 Statutory Authority

The defence of statutory authority is founded on the principle, that the law which recognizes a right, can abolish it, modify it and regulate it. Thus, the damage resulting from an act, which the legislature authorizes or directs to be done, is not actionable even though it would otherwise be a tort. When an act is done under the authority of a statue, it is a complete defence and the injured party has no remedy except for claiming such compensation as may have been provided by the statue. [21]

Thus, in *Vaughan vs. Taff Vale Railway Co.* (1860) 5 H and N 679, [14] sparks from a railway engine, of the defendants who had been authorized to run the railway, set fire to the plaintiff's wood on adjoining land. It was held that since the defendants had taken proper care to prevent the emission of sparks and they were doing nothing more than what the statute had authorized them to do, they were not liable.

In *Hammersmith Railway Co. vs. Brand*, (1869) LR 4 HL 171, [30] the value of the plaintiff's property had considerably depreciated due to the noise vibration and smoke caused by running of trains on a railway constructed under statutory powers. The damage being necessarily incidental to the trains authorized by the statue, it was held that no action lies for the same.

It is necessary that the authority conferred by the statue is exercised reasonably, with judgment and caution. Therefore, action does lie for doing that which the legislature had authorized, if it be done negligently. [15] Thus, in *Smith vs. London and South Western Railway Co.* (1870) LR 6 CP 14, [31] the railway company negligently installed grass and hedges near a rai!way line. Sparks from an engine sets the material on fire. By a heavy wind, the fire was carried to the plaintiff's cottage, 200 yards away, and the cottage was burnt as a result. Since it was a case of negligence, the defendants were held liable.

A leading case on this point is *Ramachandra Ram Nagaram Rice and Oil Mills Ltd; Gaya vs. Municipal Commissioner of Purulia Municipality,* (1943) 22 Pat 359. In this case, the plaintiff dispatched to Patna in a railway van, pure mustard oil. This tank reached Patna and about 1,000 tons were filled with this oil. The Municipal Commissioner of Purulia acting under the statue seized the oil tins on the ground that the oil was contaminated with kerosene oil. The oil was then dispatched from the station in a scavenger's truck. It was held, that the action of the defendant, in their zeal to prevent Beri, if not actuated by malice, was certainly unreasonable and negligent. It was observed, "It does not follow that the commissioner could, therefore exercise the authority thus given, in a capricious, wanton and oppressive manner. Public authorities even acting within the defined limit of their powers must not conduct themselves arbitrarily or tyrannically".

Finally, it may be noted that, the statute may give absolute or conditional authority for the doing of an act. If the authority is absolute, then even though nuisance or some other harm necessarily results, there is no liability for the same.

However, when the authority given by the statute is conditional, it means that the act authorized can be only without causing nuisance or some other harm. Thus in *Metropolitan Asylum District vs. Hill,* (1881) 6 App Cas 193, [32] the defendants were empowered to set up a small-pox hospital. They erected such a hospital in a residential area, causing the danger of infection to the residents of the area. It was held that the statutory authority in this case was conditional, and as it was causing nuisance; an injunction was issued to remove the hospital. [37]

3.5 Inevitable Accident

Such accidents which are beyond one's capacity to prevent however one has exercised ordinary care, caution and skill are called inevitable accident. It is also called unavoidable accidents. This defence is available only if the accident occurs during the prosecution of a lawful act and not when the act done is unlawful. In order to constitute an inevitable accident, it is necessary to show that the accident should not have been capable of being prevented by ordinary skill and diligence, not extraordinary skill or extraordinary diligence, by that degree of diligence and skill which is generally to be found in persons who properly discharge their duties.

If A fires at a bird but the pallet from the gun strikes a tree and rebounds and injures B in a different direction, A can take the defence of inevitable accident (*Stanley vs. Powell*, 1891 11 Q.B. 86).

If the driver is not able to control the horses which are startled by a barking dog and the plaintiff is thereby injured, the defendant will not be liable (*Holmes vs. Mather*, 1857 L.R. 10 Ex. 261).

4

Vicarious Liability

4.1 Vicarious Liability: Meaning and Examples

Vicarious liability is a form of a strict, secondary liability that arises under the common law doctrine of agency—*respondeat superior*—the responsibility of the superior for the acts of their subordinate, or, in a broader sense, the responsibility of any third party that had the "right, ability or duty to control" the activities of a violator. It can be distinguished from contributory liability, another form of secondary liability, which is rooted in the tort theory of enterprise liability.

Employers are vicariously liable, under the *respondeat superior* doctrine, for negligent acts or omissions by their employees in the course of employment (sometimes referred to as 'scope of employment'). For an act to be considered within the course of employment, it must either be authorized or be so connected with an authorized act that it can be considered a mode, though an improper mode, of performing it.

Courts sometimes distinguish between an employee's "detour" vs. "frolic". For instance, an employer will be held liable if it is shown that the employee had gone on a mere detour in carrying out their duties, whereas an employee acting in his or her own right rather than on the employer's business is undertaking a "frolic" and will not subject the employer to liability. Employer will be held liable if an employee does an authorized act in an unauthorized way.

Generally, an employer will not be held liable for assault or battery committed by employees, unless the use of force was part of their employment (such as a police officer), or they were in a field likely to create friction with persons they encountered (such as car re-possessors).

However, the employer of an independent contractor is not held vicariously liable for the tortious acts of the contractor, unless the contractor injures someone to whom the employer owes a non-delegable duty of care, as when the employer is a school authority and the injured party a pupil.

Employers are also liable under the common law principle represented in the Latin phrase, '*qui facit per alium facit per se*' (one who acts through another acts in one's own interests). That is a parallel concept to vicarious liability and strict liability, in which one person is held liable in criminal law or tort for the acts or omissions of another.

The owner of an automobile can be held vicariously liable for negligence committed by a person to whom the car has been lent, as if the owner was a principal and the driver his or her agent, *if* the driver is using the car primarily for the purpose of performing a task for the owner. Courts have been reluctant to extend this liability to the owners of other kinds of chattel. For example, the owner of a plane will not be vicariously liable for the actions of a pilot to whom he or she has lent it to perform the owner's purpose. In the United States, vicarious liability for automobiles has since been outlawed with respect to car leasing and rental in all States.

One example is in the case of a bank, finance company or other lien holder performing a repossession of an automobile from the registered owner for non-payment; the lien holder has a non-delegatable duty not to cause a breach of the peace in performing the repossession, or it will be liable for damages even if the repossession is performed by an agent. This requirement means that whether a repossession is performed by the lien holder or by an agent, the repossessor must not cause a breach of the peace or the lien holder will be held responsible.

In the United States, the question of parental responsibility generally and the issue of parental vicarious liability for the torts of their children is evolving. What is clear is that parents can be held liable for their own negligent acts, such as failure to supervise a child, or failure to keep a dangerous instrument such as a handgun outside the reach of their children.

4.2 Vicarious Liability of the State and the Question of Sovereign Immunity

In common law, the maxim [34] of law was "the king can do no wrong" therefore the king could not be sued in tort either for wrong actually authorized by it or committed by its servants, in the course of their employment. [35] The immunity of the Crown from liability, however, did not exempt the servants from liability. The individual wrongdoer was personally liable. The result was that whereas an ordinary master was liable vicariously for the wrong done by his servants, the government was not liable for a tort committed by its servants. [36] The portion has been entirely changed after the passing of the Crown Proceedings Act, 1947. [37] Now the Crown is liable for a tort committed by its servants just like a private individual.

In India, unlike the Crown Proceedings Act, 1947 we do not have any statutory provision mentioning the liability of the statue. [34] In this context, Article 300 of the Constitution of India [38] states as under:

"The Government of India may sue and be sued by the name of Union of India and the Government of a State may sue and be sued by the name of the state and may be subject to any provision which may be made by an Act of Parliament or the Legislature of such state enhanced by virtue of power conferred by the Constitution, sue or to be sued in relation to their respective affairs in the like cases as the Dominion of India and the corresponding Indian States might have sued or been sued if this Constitution had not been enacted". [39]

Article 300 thus provides that the Union of India and the States can sue and be sued, but as to the circumstances under which that can be done, [34] it points to the position prevailing before the commencement of the Constitution. Therefore, to know the present position we have to go back to the pre-Constitution days. For that, we may refer to Section 176 of the Government of India Act, 1935. That Act like the present Constitution, does not give the circumstances of the Government's liability [40] but recognizes the position prevailing before the passing of that Act. We find a similar provision in Section 32 of the Government of India Act, 1915. Finally, in Section 65 of the Government of India Act, 1858, [41] the Secretary of State in Council shall and may sue and be sued as well in India as in England by the name of the Secretary of State in Council as a body corporate and all persons and bodies politic shall and may have and take the same suits, remedies and proceedings, legal and equitable, against the Secretary of State in Council as they would have done against the East India Company.

As to the position of the East India Company prior to 1858, an important case is the decision of *Peninsular and Oriental Steam Navigation Company vs. Secretary of State for India,* (1868-69) 5 Bom HCR, App 1 P 1, where a suit was filed against the secretary of State for India in Council for the damage which was caused due to the negligence of the servants employed by the Government of India. [42] The court while looking into the liability of the East India Company drew a distinction between the sovereign and non-sovereign functions of the East India company. [40] It was held that if the act was done in the exercise of sovereign functions, the East India Company would not be liable, but if the function was a sovereign one, i.e. which could have been performed by a private individual without any delegation of power by the Government, the Company would be liable. The logic of this case was followed in *Nobin Chander Dey vs. Secretary of State for India,* ILR (1875-76) 1 Cal 11, [34] where the state was exempted from liability when the function was considered to be a sovereign one.

The Supreme Court in *State of Rajasthan vs. Vidyawati,* AIR 1962 SC 933, [15] almost overruled this test when it observed, "In this connection, it has to be remembered that under the Constitution we have established a welfare state, whose functions are not confined only to maintaining law and order, but extend to engaging in all activities including industry, public transport, state trading to name only a few of them. In so far as the State activities have such wide ramifications involving not only the use of sovereign powers but also its powers as an employer in so many public sectors, it is too much to claim that the state should be immune from the consequences of tortuous acts of its employees committed in the course of their employment as such. [43]

Unfortunately, the Supreme court in the case of *Kasturi Lal Ralia Ram Jain vs. State of U.P.,* AIR 1965 SC 1039, [44] again stated that if the act of government servant was one which could be considered to be in delegation of sovereign powers, the state would be exempt from liability.

The position which emerges from the various decisions is as follows:

1. The liability of the Union of India and the state is the same as was that of the East India Company.
2. The Government is not liable for the torts committed by its servants in exercise of sovereign powers.
3. The Government is liable for the torts which have been committed in exercise of non-sovereign powers.
4. Sovereign powers means powers which can be lawfully exercised only by a sovereign or by a person to whom such powers have been delegated. For example, functions like maintenance of defence forces, maintenance of law and order etc. Broadly speaking, such functions, in which private individuals can be engaged in, are not sovereign functions, for example, trade, business, commerce, and the welfare activities are amongst the non-sovereign functions.

Tort committed by the servants of the State in discharge of obligations imposed by law and in exercise of sovereign functions has been considered a defence in India. It is, however, necessary that the statutory functions which are exercised by the Government servant were exercised by way of delegation of the sovereign powers of the State. In case the tortious act committed by the servant has been in discharge of non-sovereign functions, the State would be liable for the same. [45]

The palpable unjustness of the decision in *Kasturilal's* case, AIR 1965 SC 1039, [46] has led to its bypassing in recent times. Today, a number of decisions of the Supreme Court have deviated from the ratio of *Kasturilal's* case. For instance, in *State of Gujarat vs. Memon Mahomed*, AIR 1967 SC 1885, and in *Smt. Basava Kom Dyamogond Patil vs. State of Mysore*, AIR 1977 SC 1749, [46] it has been held that after seizure, the position of the Government was that of a bailee. The Government, therefore, had a duty to return the property, and on its failure to do the same, it had a duty to pay compensation. [47]

Other such cases are:

1. *Peoples Union for Democratic Rights vs. Police Commissioner, Delhi,* (1990) 1 SCC 422, where the State was ordered to pay compensation to victims of police firing.
2. *Rahul Sah vs. State of Bihar,* AIR 1983 SC 1086, [15] where monetary compensation was ordered for illegal incarceration.
3. *Sabastian M. Hongray vs. Union of India,* AIR 1984 SC 1026, where exemplary damages were awarded for disappearance of two persons in military custody.
4. *Bhim Singh vs. State of J&K,* AIR 1986 SC 494, [18] where compensation was awarded for illegal arrest and detention.
5. *C. Ramkonda Reddy vs. State,* where the compensation was awarded for negligence of jail authorities in failing to ensure the safety of prisoners.
6. *Saheelia Women Resources Centre vs. Commissioner of Police, Delhi,* AIR 1990 SC 513, where the Supreme Court clearly rejected the defence of sovereign immunity.

7. *Hazur Singh vs. Jang Singh*, AIR 1973 Raj 82, where it was held that the defence of sovereign immunity is not available to State in case of illegal and wrongful acts of its employees.

In its First Report on the 'Liability of State in Tort', [37] the Law Commission of India recommended legislation prescribing State liability, as in England. It said that the Government should place itself in the same position as a private employer, and the distinction between sovereign and non-sovereign functions should not be invoked. [47] The Law Commission also recommended four exceptions to this rule:

1. Act of state.
2. Judicial act.
3. Act done in exercise of political functions such as foreign affairs, war and peace, acts in emergency etc.
4. Act done in relation to defence forces.

4.3 Liability of the Master for the Tort of His Servant

A wrongful act done by a servant in the course of his duties makes his master liable for the same as the act of the servant is deemed to be the act of the master. However, the servant is also liable.

There should be presence of two essentials to establish the liability of the master:

1. The tort was committed by the "servant".
2. The servant committed the tort in the "course of his employment".

In *Baxi Amrik Singh vs. Union of India* (1973)75 P.I.R. 1, it was held that the doctrine of liability of the master for the act of his servant is based on the maxim *respondent superior* which means "let principal be liable" and it puts the master in the same position as if he had done that himself. It also delivers validity from the maxim *qui facit per allium facit per se, which* means 'he who does an act through another is deemed in law to do it himself'.

In *Limpus vs. London General Omnibus Co.*, (1862) 1 H & C. 526), it was held that the liability arises even though the servant acted against the express instructions and for no benefit of his master.

A servant is a person implied by another to do under the directions and control of his employer. As a general rule, a master is liable for the wrong of his servant but he is not liable for the wrong of an independent contractor.

4.3.1 Distinction between a Servant and an Independent Contractor: A servant works as an agent under the control and supervision of his master regarding the weight in which the work is needed to be done whereas an independent contractor is free from such control. He undertakes to do certain work and he decides the manner himself how the work is to be accomplished. He is considered to be his own master and exercises his own discretion. An independent contractor is one who undertakes to produce a given result, so that in the actual execution of the work he is not under the order or control of the person for whom he does it and he may use his own discretion in matters not specified earlier. For example, my car driver who happens to be my servant negligently knocks down a person A, then I will be liable for that. However, when I hire a taxi and the taxi driver negligently does the same act, I will not be liable towards A as the taxi driver is only an independent contractor not my servant and he alone will be liable for the tort committed.

4.4 Liability of the Principal for the Tort of His Agent

If an agent commits a tort in performance of his duty as an agent, the liability of the principal arises for such a wrongful act. The agent is also liable because he has done the wrongful act. It is based on the general principle "Qui facit per alium facit per se", which means that the act of agent is the act of the principal. Their liability is joint and several. Where the plaintiff's husband gave some amount and cheques to his friend who was defendant bank's employee, to be deposited in the plaintiff's account and the plaintiff got no receipt for the deposit as the bank employee misappropriated the amount, the Supreme Court held that the employee when he committed the fraud, was not acting in the scope of bank's employment but in his private capacity so the defendant bank could not be made liable (*State Bank of India vs. Shyama Devi*).

4.5 Liability of Partner for Each Other's Tort

The partners have the same relationship in the law of tort as that of the principal and the agent; hence the rule of principal and agent also applies in case of their liability. If one partner in the ordinary course of business of the firm commits a tort, all the other partners are liable to the same extent as the guilty partner. The liability of each partner is joint and several. When one of the two partners of the defendant's firm acted in the course of partnership and bribed the plaintiff's clerk and induced him to make a breach of contract with the plaintiff by revealing separates to his employers business, it was held that both the partners of the firm were liable for the breach of contract committed, including the other wrongful act committed by only one of them.

5

Remoteness of Damages

It is generally perceived that consequences of a wrongful act are infinite, but in law of tort, the defendant is liable only for those consequences which are not too 'remote' from his conduct. [48] The word remote is used as the opposite of near or proximate. In other words, whatever is not the direct and immediate result of the wrongful act is a remote consequence.

In the course of judicial evolution of the concept of remoteness of damage, two main tests [21] emerged:

1. The test of reasonable foresight.
2. The test of directness.

5.1 Test of Reasonable Foresight

According to this test, if the consequences of a wrongful act could have been foreseen by a reasonable man they are not too remote. [49] This test is also called the *test of probability* which means a man is responsible for the probable consequence of his action. So, if a person commits a wrong, he will be liable only for those consequences which he could foresee, for whatever could not have been foreseen is too remote a consequence of his wrongful act.

The test of reasonable foresight emerged from the dicta of [50] Pollock C.B. in *Rigby vs. Hewit*, (1850) 5 Ex 240 and *Greenland vs. Chaplin* (1850) 5 Ex 243, wherein it was held [21] that the liability of the defendant is only for those consequences which could have been foreseen by a reasonable man placed in the circumstances of the wrongdoer.

5.2 Test of Directness

According to the test, a person is liable for all the direct consequences of his wrongful act, whether he could have foreseen them or not; because consequences which directly follow a wrongful act are not too remote. [49]

The test of reasonable foresight was acceptable to the judiciary till 1921, when Scrutton, L.J., rejected it and propounded the test of directness in Polemis and Furness Withy & Co. Ltd. (1921) 3 KB 560. In this case, a ship carried a quantity of petrol in tins. Due to leakage in those tins some of their contents collected in the hold of the ship. Owing to the negligence of the defendant servants, a plank fell into the hold and a spark was caused and consequently the ship was totally destroyed by fire. The owners of the ship were held entitled to recover, it being the direct consequence of the wrongful act although such a loss could not have been reasonably foreseen. [21]

This test was previously applied in the case of *Smith vs. London and South Western Railway Company,* (1870) LR 6 CP 14, where a railway company negligently allowed a heap of trimmings of hedges and grass to lie near a railway line. A spark from the railway engine set fire to the material, which due to high wind was carried to the plaintiff's cottage which was burnt. The defendants were held liable [51] even though they could not have foreseen the loss to the cottage.

The scope of the above test was limited by the House of Lords in *Liesbosch Dredger vs. Edison,* (1933) AC 449. [52] In this case, owing to the negligence of the defendant, [14] Dredger Liesbosch sunk. The owners of Liesbosch required it for the performance of a contract with a third party, but since they were too poor to purchase a new one, they hired one at an exorbitant rate. They sued the defendants for compensation *inter alia* for the hire charges which they had to pay from the date of the sinking to the date they could actually purchase a new dredger. [53] The House of Lords allowed damages only till the date when another dredger could reasonably have been put to work. The claim after that time was rejected. The reason why new dredger could not be purchased by the plaintiffs was their poverty and it was considered an extraneous cause and as such too remote.

The test of directness has been considered to be incorrect by the Privy Council in *Overseas Tankship (U.K.) Ltd. vs. Morts Dock and Engineering Co. Ltd.* (Wagon Mound No.1 Case), (1961) 1 All ER 404 (PC), [54] and it was held that the test of reasonable foresight is a better test. In this case, the Wagon Mound, an oil burning vessel, was chartered by the appellants and was taking fuel oil at Sydney port. At a distance of about 600 feet, the respondents, Morts Dock Company, owned a wharf, where some welding operations were going on. Due to negligence of appellant servants, a large quantity of oil was spilt on the water and carried to the respondent's wharf. Molten metal from the respondent's wharf fell on it and the resulting fire caused great damage to the wharf and equipment. It was established that such damage could not have been reasonably foreseen. [21] The appellants were not liable even though their act was the direct cause of the damage. [14]

This ruling has been approved by the House of Lords in *Hughes vs. Lord Advocate,* (1963) 1 AII ER 705 (HL). [55] In this case, the post office employees who had opened a manhole for the purpose of maintaining underground telephone equipment, left it open and unguarded though surround by paraffin lamps. A child started playing with one of the lamps, which fell into the manhole and caused a violent explosion resulting in the fall of the boy also in the hole and causing severe injuries to him. It was foreseeable that a child could get burnt by playing with the lamp, but the explosion could not be foreseen. The House of Lords held [56] that since the kind of damage was foreseeable although the extent was not, the defendant was liable.

In *Doughty vs. Turner Manufacturing Co. Ltd.,* (1964) 1 AII ER 98 (CA), the test of reasonable foresightness has been applied. In this case, the servant of the defendant let an asbestos cement cover to slip into cauldron of hot molten liquid. It resulted in an explosion causing injuries to the plaintiff, who was standing nearby. It was established that nobody could foresee that an explosion could follow by the falling of the asbestos cover into the cauldron. It was held, that the damage resulting from the explosion was not of the kind as would have been reasonably foreseen, therefore, the defendants were not liable.

In this line of application, another case is *S.C.M. (United Kingdom) Ltd. vs. W.J. Whittal & Sons* (1991) 1 QB 337, [15] where due to the negligence of the defendant's workmen, an electric cable was damaged. As a result, there was a seven hour power failure in the plaintiff's factory. The plaintiff claimed compensation for damages to materials and machines and consequent loss of production. It was held that the defendants knew that the said electric cables supplied electric current to the factories and that they could foresee the loss of production, due to power failure, therefore, they were liable for the damages.

Therefore, we can conclude that foreseeability has become the accepted test for determination of damages.

In *Smith vs. Leech Brain & Co. Ltd.* (1962) 2 QB 405 ("Eggshell Skull" case), [57] it was laid down that if the plaintiff suffers personal injury from the wrongful act of the defendant, it is no answer to the claim that the plaintiff would have suffered less injury "if he had not usually thin skull or an unusually weak heart". *A* tort feasor takes his victim as he finds him. [58]

In this case, a workman of the defendants, because of their negligence, suffered a burn injury on his lower lip which promoted cancer at the site of the burn, resulting in his death. But for the burn, the cancer might have never developed, though there was a pre-malignant condition and there was likelihood that it would have done so at some stage in his life. In an action by the widow of the deceased workman, the defendants were held liable for his death on the principle that a tort feasor must take his victim as he finds him.

Smith's case was followed in *Robinson vs. The Post Office,* (1974) 2All ER 737(CA). In this case, it was held that it was foreseeable that if a workman slipped from a ladder made slippery because of the negligence of the employer, the workman was likely to suffer injury, needing medical treatment in the form of injection of ATS. Although it was not foreseeable that the injection given even without any negligence on the doctor's part would cause encephalitis to the workman because he was allergic to the second dose of ATS, yet the Post Office were held liable on the ground that they were bound to take the plaintiff as they found him.

6

Classes of Torts

In India, tort law is a relatively new area based on common law, supplemented by codifying statutes including statutes governing damages. While India generally follows the UK approach, there are certain differences which may indicate judicial activism, hence creating controversy. Tort is breach of some duty, independent of contract which has caused damage to the plaintiff, giving rise to civil cause of action and for which remedy is available. If there is no remedy it cannot be called a tort because the essence of tort is to give remedy to the person who has suffered injury.

6.1 Types of Torts

6.1.1 Class A [59]: Personal Wrongs:

1. Wrongs affecting safety and freedom of the person: assault, battery, false impı isonment.
2. Wrongs affecting personal relations in the family: seduction, enticing away of servants.
3. Wrongs affecting reputation: slander and libel.
4. Wrongs affecting estate generally: deceit; slander of title, fraudulent competition by colorable limitation etc., malicious prosecution, conspiracy.

6.1.2 Class B [60]: Wrongs to Property:

1. Trespass: (a) to land and (b) to good. Conversion and unnamed wrongs *enjusdem generic.* Disturbance of easement etc.
2. Interference with rights analogous to property such as private franchise, patents, copyrights and trademarks.

6.1.3 Class C [60]: Wrongs to Person, Estate and Property Generally:

1. Nuisance.

2. Negligence.
3. Breach of absolute duties attached to the occupation of fixed property to the ownership and custody of dangerous things and to the exercise of certain public callings.

6.2 Classification of Torts as Given by Professor Winfield

6.2.1 Wrongs to Person:

1. Death.
2. Assault and battery.
3. False imprisonment.
4. Residuary trespass to the person.
5. Injuries affecting family relations: husband and wife; parent and child.

6.2.2 Wrongs to Reputation:

1. Defamation including slander and libel.

6.2.3 Wrongs to Property:

1. Trespass to land.
2. Conversion and other wrongs to chattel.

6.2.4 Wrongs to Person or to Property:

1. Deceit.
2. Negligence.
3. Nuisance.
4. Conspiracy.
5. Breaches of strict duties.

6.2.5 Wrongs of Interference with Freedom of Contract or of Business:

6.2.6 Abuse of Procedure:

1. Malicious prosecution and civil procedure.
2. Maintenance and champers.

6.3 Capacity to Sue and be Sued

6.3.1 Every Person May Maintain an Action in Tort Except:

1. An alien enemy.
2. A foreign State.
3. A convict.

4. A bankrupt (limited capacity).
5. A married woman (limited capacity).
6. A corporation.

6.3.2 Every Person who Commits a Tort is Liable to be Sued Except:

1. The state and its subordinates (limited immunity).
2. Foreign sovereign and ambassador.
3. Corporations (limited immunity).
4. Trade unions.

7

Doctrine of Strict Liability

7.1 Strict Liability: Meaning and Examples

In law, strict liability is a standard for liability which may exist in either a criminal or civil context. A rule specifying strict liability makes a person legally responsible for the damage and loss caused by his/her acts and omissions regardless of culpability (including fault in criminal law terms, typically the presence of *mens rea*). Under strict liability, there is no requirement to prove fault, negligence or intention. Strict liability is prominent in tort law (especially product liability), corporation law and criminal law.

In tort law, strict liability is the imposition of liability on a party without a finding of fault (such as negligence or tortious intent). The claimant only need to prove that the tort occurred and that the defendant was responsible. The law imputes strict liability to situations it considers to be inherently dangerous. It discourages reckless behavior and needless loss by forcing potential defendants to take every possible precaution. It also has the effect of simplifying and thereby expediting court decisions in these cases.

A classic example of strict liability is the owner of a tiger rehabilitation center. No matter how strong the tiger cages are, if an animal escapes and causes damage and injury, the owner is held liable.

Another example is a contractor hiring a demolition sub-contractor that lacks proper insurance. If the sub-contractor makes a mistake, the contractor is strictly liable for any damage that occurs.

A more everyday example is that of a passenger on public transport who was unable to purchase a valid ticket for the journey due to extraneous circumstances, such as being unable to purchase a ticket for whatever reason. Under strict liability, it does not matter if the ticket machine was broken, or the train was early, or there were no staff at the counter. The legal responsibility for holding a valid ticket falls on the passenger and the passenger should not have travelled without one, regardless of the circumstances.

In strict liability situations, although the plaintiff does not have to prove fault, the defendant can raise a defense of absence of fault, especially in cases of product liability, where the defense may argue that the defect was the result of the plaintiff's actions and not of the product, that is, no inference of defect should be drawn solely because an accident occurs. If the plaintiff can prove that the defendant *knew* about the defect before the damages occurred, additional punitive damages can be awarded to the victim in some jurisdictions.

The doctrine's most famous advocates were Learned Hand, Benjamin Cardozo and Roger J. Traynor.

Under English and Welsh law, in cases where tortious liability is strict, the defendant will often be liable only for the reasonably foreseeable consequences of his act or omission (as in nuisance).

Strict liability is sometimes distinguished from absolute liability. In this context, an *actus reus* may be excused from strict liability if due diligence is proved. Absolute liability, however, requires only an *actus reus*.

The concept of strict liability is also found in criminal law, though the same or similar concept may appear in contexts where the term itself is not used. Strict liability often applies to vehicular traffic offenses. In a speeding case, for example, whether the defendant knew that the posted speed limit was being exceeded is irrelevant. The prosecutor would need to prove only that the defendant was operating the vehicle in excess of the posted speed limit.

In the United States, strict liability can be determined by looking at the intent of the legislature. If the legislature seems to have purposefully left out a mental state element (*mens rea*) because they felt mental state need not be proven, it is treated as a strict liability. However, when a statute is silent as to the mental state (*mens rea*) and it is not clear that the legislature purposely left it out, the ordinary presumption is that a mental state is required for criminal liability. When no *mens rea* is specified, under the Model Penal Code (MPC), the default *mens rea* requirement is recklessness, which the MPC defines as "when a person consciously disregards a substantial and unjustifiable risk with respect to a material element".

Strict liability laws can also prevent defendants from raising diminished mental capacity defenses, since intent does not need to be proven.

7.2 Ingredients of the Rule of Strict Liability

The ordinary rule is that a person is liable for those torts which he intended to commit, or which have been committed as a consequence of his negligence. The doctrine of strict liability [61] (or no fault liability) forms an exception to this rule, whereby a person may be liable for some harm even though he is not negligent in causing the same or there is no intention to cause the harm, or sometimes he may even have made some positive efforts to avert the same.

The leading case in this regard is the decision of the House of Lords in *Rylands vs. Fletcher*, (1868) LR 3 HL 330. [62] In this case the defendant got s reservoir constructed through independent contractors, over his land for providing water to his mill. There were old disused shafts under the site of the reservoir, communicating with the mines of the plaintiff, which the contractors failed to observe and so did not block them. When the water was filled in the reservoir, it burst through the shafts and flooded the plaintiff's coal-mines. [21] Even though the defendant had not been negligent, he was held liable. L.J. Blackburn laid down the following rule: [63]

"We think that the rule of law is, that the person who for his own purposes brings on his lands and keeps there anything likely to do mischief if it escapes, must keep it in his peril, and if he does not do so is *prima facie* answerable for all the damages which is the natural consequence of its escape. He can excuse himself by showing that the escape was owing to the plaintiff's default; or perhaps that the escape was the consequence of *vis major*, or the act of God; but as nothing of this sort exists, there it is unnecessary to inquire what excuse would be sufficient.

To the above rule laid down by L.J. Blackburn, L.J. Carrinse laid down an important qualification that the liability under the rule is subject to the non-natural use of land.

The rule of strict liability, therefore, has three ingredients:

1. Some dangerous thing (i.e. a thing likely to do mischief if it escapes) must have been brought by a person on his land. [64]
2. The thing thus brought or kept by a person on his land must escape to the area outside the occupation and control of the defendant. [49]
3. It must be non-natural use of land [49] i.e. it must be some special use of land, which brings increased danger to others. For example, keeping one L.P.G. cylinder in a residential house is natural use, but storing 30 cylinders in it, is the non-natural use of land.

The application of these rules can be seen through the following cases. In *Crowhurst vs. Amersham Burial Board,* (1876) 4 EX D 5, it was held that if there is a prediction of the branches of the poisonous tree on the neighbor's land, this amount to an escape and if the cattle lawfully on the neighbor's land are poisoned by eating the leaves of the same, the defendant will be liable under the rule. It has been held in *Ponting* vs. *Noakes* (1894) 2 QB 281, that if the plaintiff's horse intrudes over the boundary and dies by nibbling the leaves of a poisonous tree there, the defendant can not be liable because there is no escape in this case. In *T.C. Balakrishan Menon vs. T.R. Subramanium,* AIR 1968 Ker 151, it was held that the use of explosives in a *maidan*, even on a day of festival is a non-natural use of land.

In respect of storage of large quantity of water for agricultural purposes, the courts in India have recognized an exception to the rule of strict liability, due to peculiar Indian conditions. Thus, in *Madras Railway Co. vs. Zamindar of Carvetnagaram,* (1874) IA 364 [64] where there was escape of water as a consequence of bursting of two ancient tanks situated on the zamindar's land, which provided water to thousands of Ryots, it was held that the rule in *Ryland vs. Fletcher,* (1868) LR 3 HL 330, was not applicable and the zamindar was not liable for the damage caused by the overflowing of water. Moreover, the defence of act of God was applicable.

Similarly, in *K. Nagireddi vs. Government of Andhra Pradesh,* AIR 1982 AP 119, the plaintiff had planted 285 fruit bearing trees on his land. As a result of seepage and percolation of water in Nagarjunasagar project constructed by the State Government, all those fruit trees absorbed excess water and died. It was held that the defendants were not liable. [51] The reason was stated to be the enormous benefits flowing from dams and irrigation, without which the land would be in wilderness or the land would be desert.

7.3 Recognized Defences of the Doctrine of Strict Liability

1. **Plaintiff's Own Default:** As held in *Pointing vs. Noakes,* (1894) 2 QB 281, where the plaintiff's horse intruded into the defendant land and died after eating some poisonous leaves.
2. **Act of God:** As held in *Nichols vs. Marsland,* (1876) 2 Ex D 1, [30] where the embankments of the plaintiff's artificial lakes gave way due to extraordinary rainfall.
3. **Consent of the Plaintiff:** As held in *N. Narayana Bhatterthippad vs. Travancore or Cochin Government,* AIR 1966 Tr. Co. 225, where the plaintiff's land was flooded by a dam, he had actively supported the commission of.

4. **Act of Stranger:** As held in *Richards vs. Lothian,* (1913) AC 263, [64] where some strangers blocked the waste pipe of a wash basin, which was otherwise in the control of the defendants, and opened the tap, thereby flooding the plaintiff's premises.
5. Statutory authority which is always a defence to an action for tort.

8

Absolute Liability

8.1 Meaning and Exceptions

Absolute liability is a standard of legal liability found in tort and criminal law of various legal jurisdictions.

To be convicted of an ordinary crime, in certain jurisdictions, a person must not only have committed a criminal action, but also have had a deliberate intention or guilty mind (*mens rea*). In a crime of *strict liability (criminal)* or *absolute liability*, a person could be guilty even if there was no intention to commit a crime. The difference between *strict* and *absolute* liability is whether the defence of a *mistake of fact* is available: in a crime of *absolute liability*, a mistake of fact is not a defence. Strict or absolute liability also can arise from inherently dangerous activities or defective products that are likely to result in harm to another, regardless of protection taken. Negligence is not required to be proven. Example, owning a pet rattle snake.

In India, absolute liability is a standard of tort liability which stipulates that where an enterprise is engaged in a hazardous or inherently dangerous activity and harm results to anyone on account of an accident in the operation of such hazardous or inherently dangerous activity—for example, in escape of toxic gas the enterprise is strictly and absolutely liable to compensate all those who are affected by the accident—such liability is not subject to any of the exceptions which operate vis-à-vis the tortious principle of strict liability under the rule in *Rylands vs. Fletcher*.

In other words, absolute liability is strict liability without any exception. This liability standard has been laid down by the Indian Supreme Court in *M.C. Mehta vs. Union of India* (Oleum Gas Leak Case). These exceptions include:

- Plaintiff's own mistake.
- Plaintiff's consent.
- Natural disasters.
- Third party's mistake.
- Part of a statutory duty.

The Indian Judiciary tried to make a strong effort following the Bhopal Gas Tragedy, December, 1984 (*Union Carbide Company vs. Union of India*) to enforce greater amount of protection to the public. The doctrine of absolute liability was therefore evolved in Oleum Gas Leak Case and can be said to be a strong legal tool against rogue corporations that were negligent towards health risks for the public. This legal doctrine was much more powerful than the legal doctrine of strict liability developed in the UK case of *Ryland's vs. Fletcher*. This meant that the defaulter could be held liable for even third party errors when the public was at a realistic risk. This could ensure stricter compliance to standards that were meant to safeguard the public.

8.2 Supreme Court's Rule of Absolute Liability

The Supreme Court propounded the rule of "absolute liability" in *M.C. Mehta vs. Union of India* (AIR 1987 SC 1086). This rule was given preference over the rule of strict liability as laid down in *Ryland vs. Fletcher*. This new rule bars all the exceptions given in *Ryland vs. Fletcher* so that the wrong doer cannot escape taking the help of the exceptions when he has deliberately established hazardous industries in and around the thickly populated areas. In this case, M.C. Mehta, a social activist and lawyer sought closure of Shri Ram Industries on the ground that the industry was manufacturing hazardous substances and was located in a densely populated area. In the mean time, when the petition was pending before the court, oleum gas leaked from one of its units and affected many people.

The observation of the court was that the rule evolved in *Rylands vs. Fletcher* was not suitable to the social and economic condition in India at that time. Moreover, the rule evolved in the 19th century when science and technology were not much developed.

The Court came up with a rule stricter than strict liability or no fault liability better known as "absolute liability" which stated, "an enterprise which is engaged in a hazardous or inherently dangerous industry which poses a potential threat to the health and safety of the persons working in the factory and residing in the surrounding areas owes an absolute and non-delegable duty to the community to ensure that no harm results to anyone on account of hazardous or inherently dangerous activity which it has undertaken...and if any harm results on account of such an activity, the enterprise must be absolutely liable to compensate for such harm and it should be no answer to the enterprise to say that it had taken all reasonable care and that the harm occurred without any negligence on its part...and such liability is not subject to any of the exceptions which operate *vis-à-vis* the tortuous principle of strict liability under the rule in *Rylands vs. Fletcher*".

Since the dangerous or hazardous activities are carried on by the enterprise solely for earning profit, the enterprise must be held strictly liable for such harms as part of the social cost for carrying on the hazardous activities. It alone has the means to discover the nature of the hazard, the guard against the hazards, device to face the danger and create waning system against the potential hazards.

Quantum of damages: The court observed that the compensation should have a deterrent effect. It should be correlated to the magnitude and capacity of the enterprise. The bigger and prosperous the enterprise is, the greater must be the quantum of compensation payable by it.

9

Public Liability, Liability Insurance and Public Liability Insurance Act, 1991

9.1 Public Liability

Public liability is part of the law of tort which focuses on civil wrongs. An applicant (the injured party) usually sues the respondent (the owner or occupier) under common law based on negligence and/or damages. Claims are usually successful when it can be shown that the owner/occupier was responsible for an injury, therefore they breached their duty of care.

The duty of care is very complex, but in basic terms, it is the standard by which one would expect to be treated whilst one is in the care of another.

Once a breach of duty of care has been established, an action brought in a common law court would most likely be successful. Based on the injuries and the losses of the applicant the court would award a financial compensation package.

In the course of managing any property, one is obliged to comply with laws and statutes administered by the government and municipal bodies. These bodies impose various liabilities of which the property owner/manager should be aware.

The most common examples of statute liability are in areas where you are required by law to effect insurance, e.g. workers' compensation and motor vehicle compulsory third party.

Property, hotel and operations managers should become familiar with the various types of contracts involved in commercial and retail activities.

The major contractual liability from an insurance viewpoint is undoubtedly found in head lease and management agreements. These require the manager or head lessee to fully maintain, repair and replace the property, if damaged, until expiration of the agreement or lease.

Furthermore, the contracts usually require an indemnity to the owner against liabilities imposed upon the business for injuries and property damage arising out of the use, occupation or management of the property.

Every contract contains covenants imposing responsibilities on one or other of the parties. These should be carefully examined to ensure they are not unduly onerous.

Owner/occupiers are required to provided a certain level of care. The duty of care is not the same for all people. It is dependent on a number of issues. To assist in establishing the duty of care required it is better to divide into groups the individuals who are on your premises and for what reasons. If we take an example of a large shopping complex the following groups of individuals would attract different levels of care.

9.1.1 Invitees: These are people who by some form you have invited into your complex. This invitation can be through marketing and advertising, or it can be implied simply because you are a shopping complex or hotel. The greatest duty of care is owed to invitees who, in the case of shopping centres and hotels, are mainly customers, contractors and sub-contractors. They are there because of the invitation you extend to them. The duty of care owed to them is relatively simple.

You must take reasonable care to ensure that the premises are safe. They in turn must take reasonable care for their own safety.

If however an invitee spends money for a service, i.e. forms a contract with you, your duty of care is enhanced. An example of this could be a games arcade where the invitee pays for a ride on a motorcycle game. If as a result of playing this game, the invitee is electrocuted, you have breached your duty of care and will most likely be found to be liable for any damages.

If, however, the reason for the electrocution was not due to your negligence but a product defect, and you have done all that is reasonably expected of an arcade owner to detect and fix this defect, you may proceed to sue the supplier of the game. This is because the supplier also owns a duty of care to the arcade owner as well as a contractual duty to provide safe and functioning equipment.

9.1.2 Licensees: These are people who enter premises with the permission of the occupier but, unlike invitees, do so without any economic advantage to the occupier. They come in the hope of doing business with you or your tenants and include such people as salesmen, commercial travelers, etc. The duty of care owed to licensees are not quite as extreme as in the case of the invitees.

9.1.3 Trespassers: These are classified as people who intrude into a property without permission. The degree of care owed to trespassers, although slight, nevertheless exists particularly in situations where a source of danger is deliberately created or where small children are involved. An example would be where live wires were left exposed after the centre had closed. If some children entered the premises for some reason, despite that reason, if they were injured, the owner of the centre would be liable.

9.1.4 Types of Claim: The most common types of claims fall into a small number of categories: (a) slips, trips and falls—these make up the majority of claims; (b) stress and anxiety, due to hold ups, elevator malfunction, etc. and (c) falling objects, i.e. striking against or struck by.

In the event a third party articulates or formulates a demand or application of damage against you, public liability insurance will cover the cost of the claim.

9.2 Liability Insurance

Liability insurance is a part of the general insurance system of risk financing to protect the purchaser (the "insured") from the risks of liabilities imposed by lawsuits and similar claims. It protects the insured in the event he or she is sued for claims that come within the coverage of the insurance policy. Originally, individuals or companies that faced a common *peril*, formed a group and created a self-help fund out of which to pay compensation should any member incur loss (in other words, a mutual insurance arrangement). The modern system relies on dedicated carriers, usually for-profit, to offer protection against specified perils in consideration of a premium. Liability insurance is designed to offer specific protection against third party insurance claims, i.e., payment is not typically made to the insured, but rather to someone suffering loss who is not a party to the insurance contract. In general, damage caused intentionally as well under contractual liability are not covered under liability insurance policies. When a claim is made, the insurance carrier has the duty (and right) to defend the insured. The legal costs of a defence normally do not affect policy limits unless the policy expressly states otherwise; this default rule is useful because defence costs tend to soar when cases go to trial.

9.3 Public Liability Insurance Act, 1991

After having two major disasters Bhopal Gas Leak disaster and Shri Ram Gas Leak tragedy Public Liability Insurance Act 1991was enacted. The view was that the victims of the handling of hazardous substance can be relieved through insurance expeditiously.

The main objective of the Public Liability Insurance Act 1991 is to provide for damages to victims of an accident which occur as a result of handling any hazardous substance. The Act applies to all owners associated with the production or handling of any hazardous chemicals.

The important features are as follows:

1. It provides for mandatory insurance for the purpose of providing an immediate relief to the persons affected by the accidents occurring while handling any hazardous substance.

2. Every industry, public or private, which handles such hazardous substances, are covered by the Act.
3. Hazardous substance stands for all such substance with its physio-chemical properties having the potential of causing harm to all living organisms including the environment.
4. The Act is based on the principle of "no fault measures".
5. There would be an absolute duty on the part of the owner to compensate any kind of damages arising out of the accidents.
6. The entire burden of paying compensation however not to exceed the paying capacity of the owner.
7. Every owner has to take one or more insurance policies providing for contracts of insurance whereby he is insured against the liability of damages arising out of accident while handling hazardous substance. In respect of already established industry, such policies have to be taken within a year.

10

Trespass

Trespass is an area of criminal law or tort law broadly divided into three groups: trespass to the person, trespass to chattels and trespass to land.

Trespass to the person historically involved six separate trespasses: threats, assault, battery, wounding, mayhem and maiming. Through the evolution of the common law in various jurisdictions, and the codification of common law torts, most jurisdictions now broadly recognize three trespasses to the person: assault, which is "any act of such a nature as to excite an apprehension of battery"; battery, "any intentional and unpermitted contact with the plaintiff's person or anything attached to it and practically identified with it"; and false imprisonment, the "unlaw[ful] obstruct[ion] or depriv[ation] of freedom from restraint of movement".

Trespass to chattels, also known as trespass to goods or trespass to personal property, is defined as "an intentional interference with the possession of personal property... proximately caus[ing] injury". Trespass to chattel does not require a showing of damages. Simply the "intermeddling with or use of...the personal property" of another gives cause of action for trespass. Since the case of *CompuServe Inc. vs. Cyber Promotions*, various courts have applied the principles of trespass to chattel to resolve cases involving unsolicited bulk e-mail and unauthorized server usage.

Trespass to land is today the tort most commonly associated with the term trespass; it takes the form of "wrongful interference with one's possessory rights in [real] property". Generally, it is not necessary to prove harm to a possessor's legally protected interest; liability for unintentional trespass varies by jurisdiction. "At common law, every unauthorized entry upon the soil of another was a trespasser"; however, under the tort scheme established by the Restatement, liability for unintentional intrusions arises only under circumstances evincing negligence or where the intrusion involved a highly dangerous activity.

In short, trespass, [65] signifies any transgression or offence against the law of nature, of society, or of the country, whether relating to a man's person or to his property. But the most obvious acts of trespass are:

1. Trespass *viet armis* or trespass to person.
2. Trespass *quare clausum fergit* or trespass to land.
3. Trespass *de bonis asportatis* or trespass to goods or chattels.

10.1 Tort against Person

The tort against person is generally visualized as the trespass to person. The principle of 'trespass' was that [66] any direct invasion of a protected interest from a positive act was actionable subject to justification. If the invasion was indirect though foreseeable or if the invasion was from an omission as distinguished from a positive act, there could be no liability in trespass. Recent developments have led to further limitations: [67] If the invasion is unintended, though direct and resulting from a positive act, there will still be no liability if the defendant conduct was reasonable, or even if it was unreasonable, if the invasion was an unforeseeable consequence (*Fowler vs. Lanning*, 1957-1 QB 426).

Further, it was held that when the injury is not inflicted intentionally but negligently, the only cause of action is negligence and not trespass. [68] Thus, only 'intended invasions' come under trespass (*Letang vs. Cooper*, 1965-1 QB 232). [51]

The three chief forms of intentional trespass are: assault, battery and false imprisonment. There are two important rules [69] of trespass: (i) That it is for the defendant to plead and prove justification and not for the plaintiff to show that the defendant's conduct was unreasonable; and (ii) that damage is not an essential element and need not to be proved by the plaintiff. The importance of the trespass lies in that it can be used for the protection of one's liberty and vindication of constitutional rights.

10.2 Battery

A "battery" is "intentional and direct application of force on another person without any lawful justification". Use of force, however, trivial, is enough; physical hurt need not be there.

Least touching of another in anger is a battery (*Cole vs. Turner*, 87ER 907). [21]

Battery requires actual contact (may be indirect) with the body of another person. Therefore, a seizing and laying hold of a person so as to restrain him, spitting in the face, [66] throwing over a chair or carriage in which another person is sitting, throwing water over a person, taking a person by the collar, causing another to be medically examined against his or her will, are all held to amount to battery.

The force may be used through any object like stick, bullet, or any other missile. Infliction of heat, light, electricity, gas, odour, etc. would probably be battery if it can result in physical injury or personal discomfort.

An unwanted kiss will be battery. Where a person pushed aside another to get in front, it may amount to battery.

Harm, voluntarily suffered, is no battery. The use of force may also be justified in pulling a drowning man out of water or forcibly feeding a hunger striking person to save his life. (*Leigh vs. Gladstone*, 1909-26 TLR 139). Harm which is unintentional or caused by pure accident is also not actionable.

10.3 Assault

Assault is an act of the defendant which causes to the plaintiff, reasonable apprehension of the infliction of battery on him by the defendant. [21] An assault is an attempt or threat to do a corporeal hurt to another, coupled with an apparent present ability and intention to do the act. [66] The menacing attitude and hostile purpose go to make the assault unlawful; [67] the actual contact is not necessary in an assault. [66]

The wrong consists of an attempt to do the harm rather than the harm being caused thereby. Pointing a loaded pistol at another is an assault. If pistol is not loaded then even it can be an assault, if pointed at such a distance that, if loaded, it may cause injury (*R. vs. S. George*, 9 C&P 483). [21] The test is whether an apprehension has been created in the plaintiff's mind that battery is going to be committed against him. If the plaintiff knows the pistol is unloaded, there is no assault. [70]

It is also essential that there should be prima facie ability to do the harm or in other words, there must be the means to carry the threat into effect. [71]

Interception of a blow aimed at plaintiff by a third person will not absolve the defendant from liability.

If the defendant intended to assault, if he had the capacity to understand the nature of his act, and he struck the plaintiff, he would be liable for assault and battery even if he did not know, because of mental disease, that what he was doing was wrong. But if the mental disease is so severe that the defendant's act of striking the plaintiff was not a voluntary act at all, he would be liable (*Morris vs. Marsden*, 1952-1 All ER 925).

10.4 Distinction between Assault and Battery

In assault, actual contact or infliction of force is not necessary though it is in a battery. Generally, assault precedes battery. Showing a clenched fist is an assault but actual striking amounts to battery. Throwing water upon a person is assault but as soon as the water falls on him it becomes battery.

It is, however, not necessary that every battery should include assault. A blow from behind, without prior knowledge of the person, results in a battery without being preceded by an assault. It may be noted that besides a civil action for an assault and battery, the criminal proceedings may also be taken against wrong doer.

Assault is defined in the Indian Penal Code, Section 351, while battery is equivalent to criminal force which is defined in Section 350, IPC.

10.5 False Imprisonment

False imprisonment consists of a total restraint on the liberty of another without any justification. Such a restraint may be either physical or by a mere show of authority. Winfield defines false imprisonment as the infliction of bodily restraint which is not expressly or impliedly authorized by law. [71] According to Winfield, both the terms 'false' and 'imprisonment' are rather misleading. False does not mean fallacious, but signifies what may be termed erroneous or wrong. Similarly, imprisonment in the ordinary sense of the term in not required. Thus, if a professor locks up his students in the classroom after the usual lecture hours or if a person is restrained from coming near his own premises, it would amount to false imprisonment.

10.5.1 Essential Elements of False Imprisonment: The essential elements of false imprisonment are as under:

1. Total restraint on the liberty of a person.
2. It should be without any lawful justification.

10.5.2 Total Restraint: Under criminal law, whether the restraint is total or partial, it is actionable under Section 340 of the Indian Penal Code, 1860 which declares that whoever wrongfully restrains any person in such manner as to prevent that person from proceeding beyond certain circumscribing limits is said to 'wrongfully confine' that person. [72] Article 339 of the Indian Penal Code declares that "'whoever voluntarily obstructs any person so as to prevent that person from proceeding in any direction in which that person has a right to proceed is said to 'wrongfully restraint' that person". [73] In this case, the restraint is not total and a person is prevented merely from going in a particular direction where he has a right to go. Under civil law however, the position is different. The tort of false imprisonment is constituted only when there is total restraint. In order to succeed in his action, the plaintiff need not prove imprisonment in its ordinary sense but must prove that there is complete deprivation of his liberty. No action will lie where he is unlawfully prevented from going in a particular direction.

10.5.3 Bird vs. Jones Case (1845): In *Bird vs. Jones Case* (1845), Justice Coleridge observed, "A prison may have its boundary large or narrow, visible and tangible or though real, still in conception only; it may itself be movable or fixed, but a boundary it must have, and that boundary the party imprisoned must be prevented from passing; he must be prevented from leaving that place, within [74] which the party imprisoning would confine him, except by prison breach. Some confusion seems to me to arise from confounding imprisonment of the body with mere loss of freedom; it is one part of the definition of freedom to be able to go wither-so-ever one pleases, but imprisonment is something more than the mere loss of this power; it includes the notion of restraint within some limit defined by a will or power exterior to our own". [75]

10.5.4 Means of Escape: If the person confined had means of escape, the charge of false imprisonment cannot be sustained. Means of escape however must be such as are intelligible to the person detained; further the means should provide a reasonable way out of detention. If the means of escape is likely to cause injury to the escaping person, it is of significance and the detention would fall within the ambit of false imprisonment.

10.5.5 Knowledge of the Plaintiff: Whether the knowledge of the plaintiff constituted an essential of the tort of false imprisonment, there has been a difference of opinion. In *Herring vs. Boyle* case (1834), it was held that such knowledge was essential. However, in *Meering vs. Graham White Aviation Company* case (1920), it was held that such knowledge was not essential, for bringing an action for false imprisonment. According to Lord Justice Atkin, "'It appears to me that a person could be imprisoned without his knowing it. I think that a person can be imprisoned while he is unconscious and in a state of drunkeness, while he is unconscious and while he is lunatic. These are cases where it seems to me that the person might properly complain if his imprisonment began and ceased while he was in that state. Of course, the damages might be diminished and would be affected by the question whether he was conscious of it or not". [76]

10.5.6 Unlawful Detention: The detention must be unlawful. Thus, if the detention is made in pursuance of power vested on the defendant by law, no action can be brought for false imprisonment. In *Garikpati vs. Araza Biksham* case, 1979, the defendants made a false report to the police that the plaintiff was responsible for setting fire to defendant's property. The police arrested the plaintiff but since the charge was false imprisonment filed by the plaintiff, the defendants were held liable as they had made the complaint without any justification. In case of false imprisonment, it is not necessary for the plaintiff to prove malice or negligence on the part of the defendant. [14] It is sufficient if he proves that false imprisonment was carried out by the defendant and if the defendant cannot establish sufficient justification, he would be liable for false imprisonment.

10.5.7 Lawful Detention: While detention is made lawfully or with sufficient justification, no action can be made for false imprisonment.

In *Robinson vs. Balmain Newferry Company Limited* case (1910), the plaintiff paid a penny for entry into the defendant's wharf as he intended to cross the river by one of the defendant's ferry boats. Finding that a boat was not due for the next twenty minutes, he wanted to go out but refused to pay another penny which was chargeable for exit. These rules of the defendant were displayed on the notice board. The plaintiff was prevented from forcing his way out of the defendant's offices and was not allowed to leave unless payment for exit was made. The plaintiff sued for damages for assault and false imprisonment. The Privy Council held that the plaintiff's suit could not be decreed. The court observed that there was not complaint that there was any excessive violence nor was there any false imprisonment at all. The plaintiff was merely called upon to leave the wharf. The manner in which he had contracted, the payment of a penny was a fair condition, and the defendants were entitled to result a forcible passage through the exit. [76]

10.5.8 Arrest by Private Person:

According to Section 43 of the Criminal Procedure Code, private person may arrest without warrant.

1. Any person committing a non-bailable and cognizable offence, [77] or
2. Any proclaimed offender.

Such a private person arresting another shall without delay hand over the arrested person to a police officer or if necessary take the arrested person in custody to the nearest police station. Arresting a person, when such an act is neither permitted by the provisions of the Criminal Procedure Code nor otherwise justified, will amount to false imprisonment. The arrest by a private person will not constitute the tort of false imprisonment even if the arrested person is acquitted subsequently.

10.5.9 Remedies:

A. Action for Damages: When person has been wrongfully detained, he can sue the person responsible for such detention by bringing action for false imprisonment and claim damages. Compensation can be claimed for loss of time, physical discomfort and inconvenience as also mental suffering, disgrace and humiliation.

B. Self-help: This is a remedy which is available to the person while he is under detention, a person is authorised to use reasonable force to effect his escape from detention, instead of waiting for legal action to set him free.

C. Habeas Corpus: The phrase *habeas corpus* literally means 'produce the body' and is a quick method of securing the release of a person under wrongful detention. The writ of habeas corpus may be issued by the Supreme Court under Article 32 or by the high courts' under Article 226 of the Constitution. The writ requires the person detaining to produce the detained person before the court and justify the detention. If the court is of the opinion that the detention is without any just or reasonable ground, it will order the immediate release of the person in wrongful detention.

With regard to difference between false imprisonment and malicious prosecution, Justice Wills, in *Austin vs. Dowling* case observed the distinction between the two as follows.

"The distinction between false imprisonment and malicious prosecution is well illustrated by the case where, parties being before a magistrate, one makes a charge against another, whereupon the magistrate orders the person charged to be taken into custody and detained until the matter can be investigated. The party making the charge is not liable to an action for false imprisonment because he does not set a ministerial officer in motion but a judicial officer. The opinion and judgement of a judicial officer are interposed between the charge and imprisonment. There is, therefore, at once a line drawn between the end of the imprisonment by the ministerial officer". [78] Thus, in malicious prosecution, imprisonment is the result of a judgement or other judicial order by a court of justice. If an unlawful detention or arrest of a person has been made by a private person or procured through a merely ministerial officer of law, rather than a judicial officer, the wrongful act would amount to false imprisonment. In malicious prosecution, the plaintiff has to prove malice on the defendant's part. In false imprisonment, the question of malice does not arise. In false imprisonment the onus lies on the defendant to plead and prove affirmatively the existence of reasonable and probable cause as his justification, whereas in malicious prosecution, the plaintiff must allege and prove affirmatively its non-existence.

11

Nuisance

11.1 Meaning and Types of Nuisance

Nuisance is a common law tort. It means that which causes offence, annoyance, trouble or injury. A nuisance can be either be public or private. A public nuisance was defined by English scholar Sir J. F. Stephen as, "an act not warranted by law, or an omission to discharge a legal duty, which act or omission obstructs or causes inconvenience or damage to the public in the exercise of rights common to all Her Majesty's subjects".

Private nuisance is the interference with the right of specific people. Nuisance is one of the oldest causes of action known to the common law, with cases framed in nuisance going back almost to the beginning of recorded case law. Nuisance signifies that the "right of quiet enjoyment" is being disrupted to such a degree that a tort is being committed.

Under the common law, persons in possession of real property (land owners, lease holders etc.) are entitled to the *quiet enjoyment* of their lands. However, this does not include visitors or those who are not considered to have an interest in the land. If a neighbour interferes with that quiet enjoyment, either by creating smells, sounds, pollution or any other hazard that extends past the boundaries of the property, the affected party may make a claim in nuisance.

Legally, the term *nuisance* is traditionally used in three ways:

1. To describe an activity or condition that is harmful or annoying to others (e.g., indecent conduct, a rubbish heap or a smoking chimney).
2. To describe the harm caused by the before mentioned activity or condition (e.g., loud noises or objectionable odors).

3. To describe a legal liability that arises from the combination of the two. However, the 'interference' was not the result of a neighbor stealing land or trespassing on the land. Instead, it arose from activities taking place on another person's land that affected the enjoyment of that land.

The law of nuisance was created to stop such bothersome activities or conduct when they unreasonably interfered either with the rights of other private landowners (i.e. private nuisance) or with the rights of the general public (i.e. public nuisance).

A public nuisance is an unreasonable interference with the public's right to property. It includes conduct that interferes with public health, safety, peace or convenience. The unreasonableness may be evidenced by statute, or by the nature of the act, including how long, and how bad, the effects of the activity may be.

A private nuisance is simply a violation of one's use of quiet enjoyment of land. It does not include trespass.

To be a nuisance, the level of interference must rise above the mere aesthetic. For example, if your neighbour paints their house purple, it may offend you; however, it does not rise to the level of nuisance. In most cases, normal uses of a property that can constitute quiet enjoyment cannot be restrained in nuisance either. For example, the sound of a crying baby may be annoying, but it is an expected part of quiet enjoyment of property and does not constitute a nuisance.

Any affected property owner has standing to sue for a private nuisance. If a nuisance is widespread enough, but yet has a public purpose, it is often treated in law as a public nuisance. Owners of interests in real property (whether owners, lessors, or holders of an easement or other interest) have standing only to bring private nuisance suits.

11.2 Essentials of Nuisance

The following are the essentials of nuisance:

1. There must be interference with the use of enjoyment of land or some right over it.
2. The plaintiff must show title to the thing with which interference takes place.
3. Damage.

11.2.1 Interference: Under this heading, two things need to be discussed: (i) injury to property, and (ii) interference with personal comfort.

Both the points are distinct, as to (i), it is enough if the defendant's conduct is unreasonable having regard to the time, locality and circumstances. As to (ii), a person must, in the interest of the public, submit to a reasonable amount of discomfort.

In *St. Helen's Smelting Co. vs. Tripping,* 35 L.I.Q.B. 66, the appellants carried on smelting works in neighbourhood. The respondent bought an estate there, and the noxious fumes from the work injured his trees, plants and cattle. Damages were awarded. The court drew a distinction between nuisance producing material causing injury to property and those producing personal discomfort or inconvenience. For personal inconveniences, it is relevant to enquire circumstances of the place where the thing complained of actually occurs. "If a man lives in a town, it is necessary that he should subject himself to the consequences of those operations of trade which may be carried on in his immediate locality, which are actually necessary for trade and commerce and for the benefit of the inhabitants of the town. If a man lives in a street where there are numerous shops, and shop is opened next door to him which is carried on in a fair and reasonable way, he has no ground of complaint because, to himself individually, there may arise much discomfort from the trade carried on in that shop. But when an occupation is carried on by one person in the neighbourhood of another, and the result of the trade or occupation is material injury to property, then unquestionably arises a very different consideration. I think that in case of that description, the submission which is required from persons living in society to that amount of discomfort which may be necessary for the legitimate and free exercise of trade of their neighbors, would not apply to circumstances the immediate result of which is sensible injury to the value of the property".

Further, in considering what is reasonable interference the law does not take into account abnormal sensitiveness in either person or property.

11.2.2 The Thing Affected: Private nuisance consists of injuries to property, whether to easements such as the obstruction of lights or rights of way, or the diversion of water courses, or the withdrawal of support from a house, or to other kinds of property, as by noise, noxious vapours, smoke or the like. In all such cases, the plaintiff, in order to maintain an action, must show some title to the thing to which the nuisance is alleged to be. Thus, a person in actual possession of the land can sue but a lodger or a guest of an occupier of any other person who is merely present on the premises or the servant of the occupier cannot sue.

11.3 Nuisance and Trespass Distinguished

1. Action of trespass owes its origin to writ of trespass, whereas nuisance originated in action on the case and hence trespass involves direct harm, whereas in nuisance harm may be consequential.
2. Trespass is a wrong to possession of land, but nuisance is a wrong to its use and enjoyment. Nuisance may be committed without in any way interfering with the possession of the plaintiff.
3. Trespass is actionable per se but nuisance is actionable only on the proof of actual damage to the plaintiff.

11.3.1 Defence to the Liability for Nuisance: The following are the defence to liability for nuisance:

1. *Volenti non fit injuria.*
2. Mistake.
3. Inevitable accident.
4. Private defence.

5. Necessity.
6. Statutory authority.

A right to continue a nuisance can be acquired by a prescription if it has been peaceably and openly enjoyed as an easement and as of right without interruption and for 20 years. It is essential that the thing to do in respect of which that right is claimed should have been a nuisance for more than 20 years.

12

Negligence

Negligence means neglect to take care. It is the omission to do something which a reasonable man is guided upon by those considerations which ordinarily regulate the conduct of human affairs, would do or doing something which a prudent and reasonable man would not do. [79] Or as stated in *Heaven vs. Pender,* (1883) 11 QBD 503, actionable negligence consists of the neglect of the use of ordinary care or skill towards a person to whom the defendant owes the duty of observing ordinary care and skill, by which neglect, the plaintiff has suffered injury, to person or property. [15]

12.1 Essential Ingredients of Negligence

There are three essential [21] ingredients of negligence in the law of torts:

1. That the defendant owed duty of care to the plaintiff.
2. That the defendant made a breach of that duty.
3. That the plaintiff suffered damage as a consequence thereof.

Duty of care means a legal duty. As to it, Lord Atkin propounded the following rule in *Donoghue vs. Stevenson,* (1932) AC 562 (HL): [80]

"The rule that you are to love your neighbour, becomes in law that you must not injure your neighbor. Who is my neighbor? You must take reasonable care to avoid acts or omissions which you can reasonably foresee would be likely to injure your neighbors. Who then is my neighbor? Persons so closely and directly affected by my act that I ought reasonably to have them in contemplation as being so affected when I am directing my minds to the acts or omissions which are called in question". [81]

It is evident from the test laid down by Lord Atkin [6] that the duty depends on the reasonable degree to foresee ability of the injury. Lord MacMillan observed in *Glasgow Corporation vs. Muir* (1943) AC 447 [82], "The standard of foresight of the reasonable man is in one sense an impersonal test...The reasonable man is presumed to be free both from over apprehension and from over confidence".

Thus, in *Rural Transport Service vs. Bezlum Bibi*, AIR 1980 Cal 165, the conductor of an over loaded bus invited passengers to travel on the roof of the bus. One of the passengers on the roof of the bus, was struck by an overhanging branch of a tree and as a consequence thereof died. It was held that there was negligence on the part of both the driver and the conductor of the bus, and the defendant was liable [83] for "inviting passengers to travel precariously on the top of an overload bus is itself a rash and negligent act".

It is also negligence to start a bus before passengers get into it, as was decided in *Ishwar Devi vs. Union of India*, AIR 1969 Del 183, where just as the deceased had placed his foot on the foot board of the bus and had not yet gone in, the conductor rang the bell and the driver started the bus. The driver made an attempt to overtake another stationary bus so closely that the deceased got squeezed between the two buses. It was held that both the driver and the conductor were rash and negligent in not taking proper care of the safety of the passengers.

In another case of negligence by Public Road Transport employees, *Sushma Mitra vs. Madhya Pradesh State Road Transport Corporation,* 1974 ACJ 87 (MP), [84] the plaintiff was resting her elbow on the window sill. A truck coming from the opposite direction hit her in her elbow as a result of which she received severe injuries. [85] It was held that the habit of resting elbow on the window of the bus is so common that it must enter into contemplation of a reasonable driver. It is duty of the driver to pass on the road at a reasonable distance from the other vehicle so as to avoid any injuries to the passengers whose limbs might be protruding beyond the body of the vehicle in the ordinary course. [83]

The converse proposition that there is no liability when injury is not foreseeable is illustrated by the case of *Glasgow Corporation vs. Muir* (1943) AC 447, where the manageress of tea rooms permitted a picnic party to have their food in the tea room. Two members of the picnic party were carrying a big urn containing six to nine gallons of tea to the tea room through a passage where there were some children. Suddenly one of the persons lost the grip of the handle of the urn and six children including the plaintiff, were injured. It was held that the manageress could not anticipate that such an event would happen as a consequence of tea urn being carried through the passage and therefore, she had no duty to take precautions against the occurrence of such an event.

This and the following cases also illustrate the proposition that reasonable foresee ability does not mean remote possibility. [86] The duty is to guard against probabilities rather than bare possibilities. Thus, in *Fardon vs. Harcourt-Rivington,* (1932) 146 LT 391, [87] the defendant left a dog inside his parked car. The dog smashed a glass panel, which injured the plaintiff. It was held that the accident being very unlikely there was no negligence in not taking a precaution against it...People must guard against reasonable probabilities but they are not bound to guard against fantastic possibilities.

In *Blyth vs. Birmingham Waterworks Co.* (1856) 11 Ex 781, due to exceptionally severe frost, a water plug installed by the defendants was damaged and as a result the plaintiff's premises were flooded. It was held that the defendants had provided against such frosts as experience would have led man acting prudently, to provide against; and they were not guilty of negligence, because their precautions proved insufficient against the effect of the extreme severity of the frost of 1855, which penetrated to a greater depth than any which ordinarily occurs south of the polar regions. [81]

Though obvious, it needs to be emphasized that mere carelessness on the part of the defendant does not entitle the plaintiff to sue him, for it has to be proved that the defendant owed a duty to care to the plaintiff. Thus, in *Bourhill vs. Young* (1943) AC 92 (HL), [6] a fishwife had just alighted from a tramcar. A speeding motor cyclist passed on to the side of the tramcar and immediately afterwards collided with a motorcar and was killed. The fishwife did not see the motor cyclist or the accident which had occurred but she simply heard the noise of the collision. In consequence, she sustained nervous shock. In her suit for damages it was held by Lord McMillan that the cyclist was under no duty to the appellant to foresee that his negligence in driving at an excessive speed and consequently colliding with a motor car might result in injury to her, for such a result could not reasonably and probably be anticipated. [88]

As to the standard of care required, it varies according to the each situation. The kind of risk determines the precautions which the defendant is expected to take. [89] Thus, in *Glasgow Corporation vs. Muir,* (1943) AC 447, poisonous berries in the defendants land looked like cherries and thus had a tempting appearance for the children. A child, aged seven, ate those berries and died. It was held that the defendants were liable for negligence as they ought to have anticipated the possibility and taken appropriate precautions.

In *Pinnamaneni Narasimha Rao vs. G. Jayaprakasu* (AIR 1990 A.P. 207), [17] the plaintiff, a student aged 17 years, suffered irreparable damage in the brain due to negligence of the surgeon and the anesthetist. In this case, a proper diagnosis was not done, and if the surgeon had not performed the operation, there was every possibility of the plaintiff being saved from the brain damage. The anesthetist was also negligent so far as he failed to administer respiratory resuscitation by oxygenating the patient with a mask\bag, which is an act of *per se* negligence in the circumstances. [15]

The court observed, "A person engaged in some particular profession is supposed to have the requisite knowledge and skill needed for the purpose and he has a duty to exercise reasonable degree of care needed in a particular case depending on the professional skill expected from persons belonging to a particular class. A surgeon or anesthetist will be judged by the standard of an average practitioner of class to which he belongs or holds himself out to belong. [83]

In *Dr. M. Mayi Gowda vs. State*, II (1996) C.P.J. 307 (Karnt.), certain persons having a joyride on an elephant in Mysore Dasara Exhibition Ground got seriously injured when the elephant became panicky in the rush hours and ran forward. It was found that the elephant had participated in such rides and festivals for 13 years. Held that there was no negligence on the part of the opposite parties who had organized the joyride. The reason of the accident was unusual and unfortunate because of the behaviour of the elephant, and therefore, the complaint was dismissed.

In *Nitin Walia vs. Union of India* (AIR 2001 Del 140), [90] a child visitor of Delhi Zoo aged 3 years put his hands inside the iron bars where a tigress was kept and his hand was crushed by the tigress. It was held that the zoo authorities should have put iron mesh on the rods and were liable in damages for injury and the child was not guilty of any contributory negligence.

In *State of Haryana vs. Smt. Santra* (AIR 2000 SC 1488), the question concerned as to what damages are recoverable in case of unwanted pregnancy resulting from medical negligence in sterilization operation. In this case, the plaintiff, a poor labourer women having seven children, became pregnant despite a sterilization operation performed on her in a government hospital and she gave birth to a female child. In the suit she claimed as damages the expenses needed for bringing up the unwanted child.

The Supreme Court noticed that there was no unanimity on this point in different countries but upheld the plaintiff's claim both against the doctor and the Government for damages for rearing up the child up to the age of puberty. In holding so, the court observed that "the damage for the birth of an unwanted child may not be of any value for those who are already living in affluent conditions but those who live below the poverty line or who belong to the labour class who earn their livelihood on daily basis by taking up the job of an ordinary labour, cannot be denied the claim for damages on account of medical negligence".

In India, a legal practitioner (an advocate, *vakil* or attorney of any High Court, a pleader, *mukhtar* or revenue agent) is liable for any negligence in the conduct of his professional duties. In *M. Veerappa vs. Evelyn Squeria* (AIR 1988 SC 506), the Supreme Court held that an advocate who has been engaged to act is clearly liable for negligence to his client.

In *Raman Services Private Ltd. vs. Subhash Kapoor* (AIR 2001 SC 207), the apex court held that if an advocate fails to appear due to strike call given by the bar, he can be made liable for the costs which the litigant has to pay for setting aside an *ex-parte* decree. The litigant who suffers entirely on account of his advocate's non-appearance in the court, has also the remedy to sue the advocate for damages. [91]

In *S. Dhanaveni vs. State of Tamil Nadu* (AIR 1947 Mad 257), the deceased slipped into a pit filled with rainwater in the night. He caught hold of a nearby electric pole to avert a fall. Due to leakage of electricity in the pole, he was electrocuted. The respondent maintained that the electric pole was a negligent act and was liable for death of the deceased. [92]

In *Shyamlal Baran Saha vs. State of W.B.* (AIR 1998 Cal. 203), the plaintiff, a young boy, was standing in a queue for purchasing ticket of a cricket match. Arrival of very large number of people into the queue ended in a stampede. The boy was trampled under the feet of panic stricken crowd. The defendants, Cricket Association and State Government were held liable in negligence for breach of their unlawful duties towards the plaintiff. The principle of *Res ipsa loquitur* clearly applies here.

12.2 Contributory Negligence

There are some circumstances when a person who has suffered an injury will not be able to get damages from another because his own negligence has contributed to his injury; every person is expected to take reasonable care of himself. Dr. John G. Flemming opines, "Negligence is conduct that fails to conform to the standards required by law for safeguarding others (actionable negligence) or oneself (contributory negligence) against unreasonable risk of injury". When the plaintiff by his own want of care contributes to the damage caused by the negligence or wrongful conduct of the defendant, he is considered to be guilty of contributory negligence.

As for example, when a person walking along the road, tries to cross the road all of a sudden and is hit by a moving vehicle, he is guilty of contributory negligence. [21] In this case, the defendant could completely escape his liability for the accident, on account of the plaintiff's negligence which contributed to his injury.

In *Rural Transport Service vs. Bezlum Bibi* AIR 1980 Cal 165, [17] as both the plaintiff and defendant were equally at fault, there was appointment of liability. The conductor of a bus invited passengers to travel on the roof of the bus, and one of the passengers travelling on the roof was hit by the branch of a tree and fell down and got killed after the driver swerved the bus to the right to overtake a cart. There was not only negligence on the part of the conductor and on the part of the driver (who ignored the fact that there were passengers on the roof and tried to overtake a cart) but also contributory negligence on the part of the passengers. There could be three situations regarding the liability for negligence. The three situations [84] are as follows:

1. If it were the defendant, the plaintiff can recover in spite of his own negligence (*Davies vs. Mann*).
2. If it were the plaintiff, he cannot recover in spite of the defendant's negligence (*Butterfield vs. Forester* 1809 11 East 60).
3. If it were both plaintiff and defendant, the plaintiff can recover but there will be apportionment of liability i.e. the damages will be apportioned as between them according to the degree of their fault. According to Winfield, where the plaintiff's negligence was so closely implicated with the defendant's negligence so as to make it impossible to determine whose negligence was the decisive cause, the plaintiff cannot recover. [93]

12.3 Rules to Determine Contributory Negligence

Whether there is contributory negligence or not has to be determined by the following rules: [94]

1. What the plaintiff's negligence means? Negligence of the plaintiff in relation to the defence of contributory negligence does not have the same meaning as is assigned to it as a tort of negligence. Here, plaintiff's negligence does not mean breach of duty towards the other party but it means absence of due care on his part about his own safety (*Bhagwat Swarup vs. Himalaya Gas Co.*, AIR 1985 H.P. 41).
2. Plaintiff's negligence must be the operative cause of the accident: It is not enough to show that the plaintiff did not take due care of his own safety. It has also to be proved that it is his lack of care which contributed to the resulting damage. If the defendant's negligence would have caused the same damage even if the plaintiff had been careful and the plaintiff's negligence is not the operative cause of accident, the defence of contributory negligence cannot be pleaded (*Jones vs. Livox Quarries Ltd.*, 1952 2 QB 608).
3. Test of a prudent man: To be guilty of contributory negligence, the plaintiff should not have acted like a

prudent man. If he has taken as much care as a prudent man has taken in similar situation, there is no contributory negligence. [95] Thus, merely resting one's elbow on a window sill of the bus going on a highway does not amount to contributory negligence (*Sushma Mitra vs. M.P.S.R.T. Corporation,* AIR 1974 M.P. 68). [21]

4. Doctrine of alternative danger: [94] Sometimes the plaintiff is permitted to take risk where some dangerous situation has been created by the defendant and in such a case he will not be considered to be guilty of contributory negligence. The judgement of the plaintiff should not, however, be rash (*Jones vs. Boyce,* 1816-1 Stark, 493).
5. Presumption that others are careful/statutory negligence: Such a presumption may be raised in many a cases and the plaintiff not guarding against the act of negligence of the defendant is not liable of contributory negligence in such a case. There are many circumstances when the plaintiff can take for granted that the defendant will be careful (*Gee vs. Metropolitan Railway Co.*, 1873-8 QB 161).
6. Contributory negligence of children: What amounts to contributory negligence in the case of an adult may not be so in the case of a child because a child may not be able to appreciate and understand certain danger [21] (*Motias Costa vs. Roque Augustinho Jacinto*, AIR 1976 Goa 1).
7. Doctrine of identification (imputed contributory negligence): The defence of contributory negligence can be taken not only when the plaintiff himself has been negligent but also when there is negligence on the part of his servant/agent. Thus, if I am taking the service of an independent contractor and he has been negligent, I would be identified with the independent contractor and met with the defence of contributory negligence (*Darshani Devi vs. Sheo Ram*, 1987 ACJ 931).

12.3.1 The Last Opportunity Rule: How far contributory negligence is a defence?

At common law, contributory negligence was a complete defence, and the negligent plaintiff could not claim any compensation from the defendant (*Butterfield vs. Forrester*). That caused a great hardship to the plaintiff because of slight negligence on his part and he may lose his action against the defendant who was more to blame. The courts modified the rule and introduced the so called rule of 'last opportunity' or 'last chance'.

When an accident happens through the combined negligence of two persons, he alone is liable to the other who had the last opportunity of avoiding the accident by reasonable care. [96]

In *Davies vs. Mann,* [94] the plaintiff fettered the forefeet of his donkey and left it in a narrow highway. The defendant was driving his wagon too fast and the donkey was run over and killed. In spite of his own negligence, the plaintiff was entitled to claim compensation because the defendant had the last opportunity to avoid the accident.

In *British Columbia Electric Co. vs. Loach*, (1916) 1 AC 719, the defendant who had not in fact the last opportunity to avoid the accident, will nevertheless be liable if he would have that opportunity but for his negligence".

The rule of last opportunity also was very unsatisfactory because the party whose act of negligence was earlier, altogether escaped the responsibility and whose negligence was subsequent was made wholly liable even though the resulting damage was the product of the negligence of both the parties. [21] The Maritime Convention Act, 1911 remedied the position in maritime collisions. Subsequently, the Law Reform (Contributory Negligence) Act, 1945 covered all the cases of contributory negligence. According to these Acts, when both the parties are negligent and they have contributed to some damage, the damage will be apportioned as between them according to the degree of their fault. [21] The same is considered to be the position in India as well.

12.3.2 Position in India: In *Union of India vs. Lalman Badri Prasad*, AIR 1954 VP 17, [97] Krishnan, C.J. said, "No doubt there is no corresponding statute (viz. Contributory Negligence Act, 1945 of England) in our country but the basic principle is of equity...It is dangerous to lay down the rule of all-or-nothing in cases where responsibility is divided and can be correctly apportioned". The Kerala Torts (Miscellaneous Provisions) Act, 1976 contains provisions for apportionment of liability in case of contributory negligence (Section 8).

In India, thus, contributory negligence has been considered as a defence to the extent plaintiff is at fault. Thus, if in an accident the plaintiff is as much at fault as the defendant, the compensation to which he would otherwise be entitled will be reduced by 50 percent. [94] (*Vidya Devi vs. M. P. State R.T.C.*, AIR 1975 MP 89).

According to the Motor Vehicle Act, 1988, a fixed sum in case of death and a fixed sum in case of permanent disability, of the accident victim has to be paid. In such a case, the defence of contributory negligence cannot be pleaded.

12.3.3 Theories of Contributory Negligence: Various theories have been advanced by jurists as to the basic principle of contributory negligence. Some of the important theories [84] are:

1. Penal theory.
2. Public policy.
3. Principle of joint tort feasors.
4. *Volenti non fit injuria.*
5. Causation.

12.4 *Res Ipsa Loquitur*

In the law of torts, for pleading the tort of the negligence, the general rule is that the 'plaintiff' has to prove the following: [21]

1. That the defendant owed duty of care to the plaintiff.
2. The defendant made a breach of that duty.
3. Plaintiff suffered damage as a consequence thereof.

Thus, the initial burden of making out at least a *prima facie* case of negligence as against the defendant lives heavily on the plaintiff. There are, however, certain cases when the plaintiff need not prove negligence on the part of the defendant, [17] and the presumption of negligence is drawn from the facts of the case according to the maxim 'res ipsa loquitur' which means 'the thing speaks for itself'. [21] Here, the burden of proof shifts on the defendants, who now has to rebut the presumption of his negligence.

There are two essentials for invoking the doctrine of 'res ipsa loquitur':

1. The accident explains only one thing and that is that the accident could not ordinarily occur unless the defendant had been negligent. [86]
2. That the cause of mischief was at the material time exclusively under the control or management of the defendant. [15]

The maxim is a rule of evidence, and the defendant can still escape his liability by affirmatively proving that there was no negligence on his part.

The leading case in this regard is *Municipal Corporation of Delhi vs. Subhagwanti,* AIR 1966 SC 1750, [98] involving the collapse of a clock tower belonging to the Municipal Corporation of Delhi and was exclusively under its control. It was 80 years old, while its normal life was to have been only 40-45 years, having regard to the kind of mortar used. There were also cracks in the structure which the Municipal Corporation of Delhi failed to repair. In these circumstances, the Supreme Court held [99] that the fall of the clock tower tells its own story in raising an inference of negligence on the part of the defendant. Since the defendants could not prove absence of negligence on their part, they were held liable.

Similarly, in *Nirmala vs. Tamilnadu Electricity Board,* AIR 1984 Mad 201, [21] the plaintiff's husband, was electrocuted due to the falling of high tension wires of 440 watts. It was held that the mere fact that the high tension wire had snapped and fallen, raised a presumption of negligence on the part of the defendants in maintaining those wires. Moreover, no elementary precaution of periodical inspection of wires had been taken by the defendants. It was held to be a clear case of *res ipsa loquitur*, and the defendants having failed to rebut the presumption of negligence, were held liable.

In *Gobald Motor Services Ltd. vs. Veluswami,* AIR 1962 SC 1, [100] the accident occurred when the bus went off the road, and hit a tree. From these circumstances, the Supreme Court raised the presumption that the accident had occurred due to the negligence of the driver.

In *Byrne vs. Boadle,* 1963 2 H&C 722, the plaintiff was going in a public street when a barrel of flour fell upon him from the defendant's warehouse window. It was held that the fact that its falling is prima facie evidence of negligence and the plaintiff who was injured by it is not bound to show that it could not fall without negligence, but if there are any facts inconsistent with negligence it is for the defendant to prove them.

If the defendant is able to prove that what apparently seems to be negligence was due to some factors beyond his control he can escape the liability. Thus, in *Nagamani vs. Corporation of Madras,* AIR 1956 Mad 56, [99] an iron post fell for unknown reasons on a passersby. The presumption of negligence on the part of the Corporation was raised but the Corporation was able to rebut the presumption by proving that the steel column which had fallen had been erected only 30 years ago whereas it had a normal life of 50 years, and that the columns were securely fixed and that occasional inspection of the pillar including one made a month before the accident had indicated no signs of such danger. The Corporation, therefore, was held not liable.

13

Defamation

13.1 Defamation: Meaning and Types

Defamation is the communication of a false statement that harms the reputation of an individual person, business, product, group, government, religion, or nation.

Under common law, to constitute defamation, a claim must generally be false and have been made to someone other than the person defamed. Some common law jurisdictions also distinguish between spoken defamation, called slander, and defamation in other media such as printed words or images, called libel.

False light laws protect against statements which are not technically false but misleading.

In some civil law jurisdictions, defamation is treated as a crime rather than a civil wrong. The United Nations Commission on Human Rights ruled in 2012 that the criminalization of libel violates freedom of expression and is inconsistent with Article 19 of the International Covenant on Civil and Political Rights.

A person who defames another may be called a "defamer", "famacide", "libeler" or "slanderer".

13.1.1 Slander: The common law origins of defamation lie in the torts of "slander" (harmful statement in a transient form, especially speech), each of which gives a common law right of action.

Libel and slander both require publication. The fundamental distinction between libel and slander lies solely in the *form* in which the defamatory matter is published. If the offending material is published in some fleeting form, as by spoken words or sounds, sign language, gestures and the like, then this is slander.

13.1.2 Libel: Libel is defined as defamation by written or printed words, pictures, or in any form other than by spoken words or gestures. The law of libel originated in the 17th century in England. With the growth of publication came the growth of libel and development of the tort of libel.

There are several ways a person must go about proving that libel has taken place. For example, in the United States, the person must prove that the statement was false, caused harm, and was made without adequate research into the truthfulness of the statement. These steps are for an ordinary citizen. For a celebrity or a public official, the person must prove the first three steps *and* that the statement was made with the intent to do harm or with reckless disregard for the truth, which is usually specifically referred to as "proving malice".

13.2 Important Elements of Defamation

Defamation is an actionable tort which causes injury to the reputation of a person. In *Dixon vs. Holden*, (1869) LR7 Eq 488, it was stated that a man's reputation is related as his property and if possible it may prove more valuable than any property. The meaning of reputation must be taken as what others think of a person. Defamation is defined by Winfield as, "publication of a statement which tends to lower the person's estimation among the right thinking members of the society in general or which makes them avoid or shun that person".

There are four important elements of defamation:

1. The words must be defamatory.
2. The words must relate to the plaintiff.
3. The words must be published in any manner.
4. The words must be false.

The statement of such nature as may create feeling of hatred, contempt, ridicule, fear, dislike or disesteem towards any person is said to be defamatory.

In *Sim vs. Stretch*, (1936) 2All ER 1237 (HL), the fact was that the plaintiffs housemaid left service to join the defendant.

Through a telegram, the defendant wrote "Edith has resumed her service with us today. Please send her possessions and the money you borrowed, also her wages. The plaintiff claimed damages on the ground of defamation as the words implied the plaintiff's financial difficulties which led him to borrow money from his servant. It was held that there is no reason to award damages as these words convey no defamatory meaning.

Sometimes the latent or secondary meaning may be considered defamatory however the outlook of the statement may not be defamatory. Such defamation is known as an "*innuendo*".

In *Capital and Counties Bank vs. Henty and Sons,* (1882) 74AC741, in a dispute between Henty and Sons who used to receive cheques drawn on various branches of Capital and Counties Bank. A large number of circulars were sent by the defendants to their customers stating that they would not receive payment in cheques drawn on any of the branches of the Bank. The Bank sued Henty and Sons and alleged that it was suggestion of an insolvency of the bank. The court held that the words of the circular should be taken in their natural sense which did not convey the supposed imputation and the reasonable people would not understand it in the sense of the *innuendo* suggested hence no damages were awarded.

In *Cassidy vs. Daily Mirror Newspapers Ltd.*, (1929) 2KB331, it was noted that in the law of torts the intention to defame was not necessary. It was held that the words conveying defamatory meaning and damages were awarded.

Defamation is an injury to a man's reputation which is a right *in rem*. Reputation for the purpose of law of torts is that of an individual and not a class of persons. In *Eastwood vs. Homes*, (1858) 1F & F 347, it was held that when the words refer to a group of individuals or a class or persons, no member of that group or class can sue unless he can prove that the words could reasonably be considered to be referring to him. Thus, a man who wrote that all lawyers were thieves no lawyer can sue him unless there was something to point to a particular individual.

Publication in defamation means making the defamatory matter known to some person other than the person defamed. In *Nemichand vs. Khemrai*, AIR 1973 Raj 240, the printed material was never made public as it was lying in the godown, so there was no publication.

The communication between husband and wife does not constitute publication. In the eyes of law, husband and wife are one person and the communication of a defamatory matter from the husband to the wife or vice versa is no publication (*T.J. Ponner vs. M.C. Verghese*, AIR 1970 SC 1876).

There are three defenses to an action for defamation:

1. **Justification or Truth:** A complete defense as it has been stated in *McPherson vs. Daniels* (1929) 10B and C263, 272, "the law will not permit a man to recover damages in respect of an injury to a character which he either does not ought not to possess".
2. **Fair Comment:** On matters of public interest, available to authors, editors, critics etc. the three essential are:

- It must be a comment, i.e. an expression of opinion rather than an assertion of fact.
- It must be fair.
- It must be a matter of public interest.

3. **Privilege**: There are certain occasions when the law recognizes that the right of free speech outweighs the plaintiff's right to reputation: the law treats such occasions to be "privileged" and a defamatory statement made on such occasions is not actionable. Absolute privilege is an absolute defence. It is available in matters of such extreme public importance that nothing can defeat it, not even malice.

   Absolute privilege is recognized in the following cases:

1. Article 105(2) of Indian constitution provides that:

- Statement made by the member of either house of Parliament in Parliament.

- The publication by or under the authority of either house of Parliament of any report, paper, votes or proceedings, cannot be questioned in the court of law.

2. In judicial proceedings there can be no against judges, counsels, witnesses or parties for words written or spoken in the course of any proceedings before any court recognized by law, even though the words written or spoken were written or spoken maliciously, without any justification or excuse. However, a remark by a witness which is wholly irrelevant to the matter of enquiry is not privileged as held in *Jiwan Mal vs. Lachman Dass* (1926) 27 PLR 351.
3. A statement made by one officer of the state to another in the course of official duty is absolutely privileged for reasons of public policy.

As to qualified privilege, its chief distinguishing feature from the aforesaid defense is that it is necessary that the statement must have been without malice. The two essentials of this defense are:

- The statement must be made on a privileged occasion, i.e. it was in discharge of duty of protection of an interest: or if a fair report of Parliamentary, judicial or other public proceedings.
- The statement must be made without malice.

14

Malicious Prosecution

14.1 Meaning Malicious Prosecution

Unsuccessful criminal proceeding instituted maliciously and without reasonable and probable cause is called malicious prosecution and if such prosecution causes damage to the party prosecuted, it becomes a tort for which action can be brought in the court.

Malicious prosecution is a common law intentional tort—like the tort of abuse of process—and its elements include: (a) intentionally (and maliciously) instituting and pursuing (or causing to be instituted or pursued) a legal action (civil or criminal) that is, (b) brought without probable cause and (c) dismissed in favor of the victim of the malicious prosecution. In some jurisdictions, the term "malicious prosecution" denotes the wrongful initiation of criminal proceedings, while the term "malicious use of process" denotes the wrongful initiation of civil proceedings.

Criminal prosecuting attorneys and judges are protected from tort liability for malicious prosecution by doctrines of prosecutorial immunity and judicial immunity. Moreover, the mere filing of a complaint cannot constitute an abuse of process. The parties who have abused or misused the process, have gone beyond merely filing a lawsuit. The taking of an appeal, even a frivolous one, is not enough to constitute an abuse of process. The mere filing or maintenance of a lawsuit, even for an improper purpose, is not a proper basis for an abuse of process action.

14.2 Cases

Declining to expand the tort of malicious prosecution, a unanimous California Supreme Court in the case of *Sheldon*

Appel Co. vs. Albert & Oliker, 47 Cal. 3d 863, 873 (1989) observed, "While the filing of frivolous lawsuits is certainly improper and cannot in any way be condoned, in our view the better means of addressing the problem of unjustified litigation is through the adoption of measures facilitating the speedy resolution of the initial lawsuit and authorizing the imposition of sanctions for frivolous or delaying conduct within that first action itself, rather than through an expansion of the opportunities for initiating one or more additional rounds of malicious prosecution litigation after the first action has been concluded".

In *A. Brath vs. N.E. Ry.*, (1886) 1Q.B.D. 440, 445, Per Bowen, L.J., it was laid, "In an action for malicious prosecution the plaintiff has to prove, first, that he was innocent and that his innocence was pronounced by tribunal before which the accusation was made; secondly, that there was want of reasonable and probable cause for the prosecution; or, as it may be otherwise stated, that the circumstances of the case were such as to be in the eye of the judge inconsistent with the existence of reasonable and probable cause; and lastly, that the proceedings of which he complains were initiated in a malicious spirit that is from an indirect and improper motive, and not in furtherance of justice".

Through the following leading cases on malicious prosecution, the essentials of malicious prosecution can be drawn. The cases are *Singh vs. Badri Sah*, A.I.R. 1926 P.C. 46: (1926) 30 C.W.N. 866: *Nagendra Nath Ray vs. Basanta Das* Bairagya, 1930 57 C.W.N. 25, 29; *G.J. Khona vs. K. Damodaran*, A.I.R. 1970 Kerala 229, 234; *C. Dakshinamurthy vs. K. Venkata Swamy Chettiar*, 1972 1 M.L.J. 160: 84 L.W. 813, *Ramesh Chandra vs. Jagannath*, A.I.R. 1975 Orissa 121; *Surat Singh vs. Delhi,* M.C. A.I.R. 1989 Delhi 51 and *K.T.V. Krishnan vs. P.T. Govindam*, AIR 1989 Ker. 83.

The essentials for a suit for damages for malicious prosecution are as under:

1. That the prosecution brought by the defendant.
2. That the prosecution had no reasonable and probable base.
3. That the act of defendant was malicious and had no intention to carry the law into effect.
4. That the prosecution must have ended in favour of the plaintiff.
5. That the plaintiff suffered as a result of prosecution.

The ingredients were held to be necessary to prove the tort of malicious prosecution.

Prosecution: It means initiation of proceedings in a Court charging a person with a cry (Sections 107 and 108 CrPC), causing damage to the plaintiff. The word prosecution strictly refers to criminal proceedings.

Favourable Termination of the Prosecution: The plaintiff has to prove that the prosecution ended in his favour while the prosecution was pending; he has no right to sue again if he has been convicted.

Absence of Reasonable and Probable Cause: It is the plaintiff who must prove that there was lack of reasonable cause for his prosecution. The reasonable and probable cause as defined by house of Lords is, "an honest belief in the guilt of the accused based upon a full conviction founded upon reasonable grounds of existence of a state of circumstances which, assuming them to be true, would reasonably lead any ordinarily prudent and cautious man placed in the position of the accuser, to the conclusion that the person charged was probably guilty of the crime imputed". The burden of proof to show that there was no reasonable ground for the prosecution lies upon the plaintiff.

Malice: Malice is the central point of the action for malicious prosecution. It should be *malice infact* as distinguished from *malice in law*. Malice infact stands for the defendant that action was initiated either by ill will or improper motive. Malice means the presence of some improper and wrongful motive that is an intent to use the legal process in question for something other than its legally appointed or appropriate purpose (*Jogendra vs. Lingaraj*, A.I.R. 1970 Orissa 91 100; *State of Bihar vs. Rameshwar Prasad*, A.I.R. 1980 PAT. 267).

15

Pleadings Related to Law of Torts

Action in torts covers various phase of human activities, specially slanderus and libelous and other defamatory acts including action in negligence. In modern times, the tortuous liability have grown in wide proportions and it also takes within its fold, the marriage relationship and the liability of the States, for wrongful acts against public servants, for obstruction of way, for obstruction to the use of water for irrigation, for public nuisance, for wrongful sale of plaintiff's movable and immovable properties, for damage of wrongful seizure, for damage of breach of contract, for damage for loss caused, for damage of libel, for damage for malicious prosecution, for damage for malicious civil proceedings, for damage for infringement of copyright, for injury of person, for damage for trespass, for trespass and illegal attachments, for recovery of damages and mischief, for damage on account of dog bite, for damage against doctor for negligible act, for damage against contractor for defective construction, for damages by landlord against his tenant for injury caused, etc.

For filing the suit under the law of tort one has to frame pleadings in view of the provisions as laid down under order VI, Rule 1 of the Code of Civil Procedurc 1908, that the pleading has been defined and shall mean plaint or written statement and under Rule 2(1), pleading to state material facts and not evidence. Every pleading shall contain only a statement in a concise form of the material facts on which the plaintiff in the pleadings of plaint and defendant in the pleadings of their written statement relies of his claim or defence as the case may be but not the evidence by which they are to be proved.

Every pleading shall when necessary, be divided into paragraphs, numbered consecutively, each allegation being, so far as convenient, be contained in separate paragraphs and dates, sums and numbers shall be expressed in a pleading in figure as well as in words.

As regards the conditions precedent for the performance or occurrence for getting appropriate relief under the law of torts, each party is required to place in concise form, all the material facts before the competent court of jurisdiction by way of framing of a suit as envisaged under Order II of the C.P.C. And every suit shall as far as practicable, be framed so as to afford ground of final decision upon the subject in dispute and to prevent further litigation concerning these.

Under Order II, Rule 2 of the C.P.C, every suit shall include the whole of the claim which the plaintiff is entitled to make in respect of cause of action within the jurisdiction of any court. Every suit shall be instituted by presenting plaint in duplicate to the court under Order IV of C.P.C. Every plaint shall comply with the rules contained in Order VI, so far as they are applicable.

And in all cases in which the party pleading relies on any misrepresentation, fraud, breach of trust, willful default or under influence and in all other cases in which particulars may be necessary, shall be stated in the pleading.

Every pleading shall be signed by the plaintiff or defendant as the case may be and his advocate. In view of the provisions as laid down under Order VII of the C.P.C., the plaint shall contain the following particulars:

1. Name of the court in which the suit is brought.
2. Name, description and place of residence of the plaintiff.
3. Name, description and place of residence of the defendant, so far as they can be ascertained.
4. Where the plaintiff or defendant is a minor or a person of an unsound mind, a statement to that effect.
5. Facts constituting the cause of action and when it arose.
6. Facts showing that the court has jurisdiction.

7. Relief which the plaintiff claims.
8. Where the plaintiff has allowed a set-off or relinquished a portion of his claim, the amount so allowed or relinquished.
9. A statement of the value of subject-matter of the suit for the purposes of jurisdiction and of court fees, so far as the case admits.

It is necessary to mention in the plaint the facts constituting the cause of action and when and where it arose. Cause of action means the facts or combination of facts which give rise to a right of action, the right of saying for realization of the relief arising out of the infringement.

Order II, Rule 3 provides joinder of cause of action in certain cases. Order VII, Rule 7 provides that every plaint shall state specifically the relief which the plaintiff claims either simply or in the alternative. A person entitled to more than one relief in respect of same cause of action may sue for all or any of such reliefs but if he omits except with the leave of the court, to sue for all such reliefs, he shall not afterwards, sue for any relief so omitted.

Order VI, Rule 15 provides that every pleading shall be verified at the foot of the plaint by the party or by one of the parties.

The person verifying shall specify by reference to numbered paragraphs of the pleadings of the plaint or written statement what he verifies of his own knowledge and what he verifies upon information received and believed to be true.

The verification shall be signed by the person making it and shall state the date and place which and where it was signed. The person verifying the pleadings shall also furnish an affidavit in support of his pleadings of plaint or written statement. What a plaint should contain is set out in Order VII, Rule 1 of the C.P.C. and what a written statement, set off and counter claim should contain, is set out in Order VIII of the C.P.C.

The plaint or written statement should contain as per nature and claim of several types of suit as the case may be.

Endnotes

1. http://www.contentcarry.com/all-india-bar-examination-aibe-4-sample-question-paper/14951.
2. Student papers, Amity University, March 5, 2014.
3. http://zenitheducation.net/ugcnotes/law-e.pdf.
4. Student papers, Gujarat National Law University, September 26, 2012.
5. http://www.redress.org/downloads/publications/indianseminarreport.pdf.
6. Cross-reference citation name: *Rajkot Municipal Corporation vs. Manjuben Nakum and Others*", Financial Law Reporter, April 30, 2011.
7. http://indiankanoon.org/doc/702892.
8. http://www.delhicourts.nic.in/oct07/Gatakala%20%20Venkateswarlu%20Vs.%20UOI.pdf.
9. http://www.getthroughquides.co.uk/forum/archive/index.php/t-164.html?
10. http://indiankanoon.org/doc/321930.
11. http://www.hohmann-rechtsanwaelte.de/rechtsvorschriften/contract-Act-1872.pdf.
12. http://www.authorstream.com/presentation/tabrezahmad-254830-quasi-contract-education-ppt-powerpoint.
13. http://www.indiankanoon.org/doc/68140.
14. http://archive.org/stream/selectionofcases00amesuoft/selectionof cases00amesuoft_djvu.txt.
15. http://www.du.ac.in/fileadmin/DU/Academics/course_material/2012/30812_1_LawTorts.pdf.
16. http://www.grrajeshkumar.com/class-notes-on-law-of-torts-1st-sem-3-year-ll-b.
17. http://consumereducation.in/lawtorts.pdf.
18. http://research.uniraj.ac.in/synopsis/law/sahadev%20Dan/part1.pdf.
19. http://blog.legalbird.net/damnum-sine-injuria.html.

20. http://consumereducation.in/lawtorts.pdf.
21. http://kamkus.org/pdf/LLB_1yr/Code-103.pdf.
22. Student papers, Gujarat National Law University, September 26, 2012.
23. Student papers, Gujarat National Law University, September 26, 2012.
24. Student papers, Gujarat National Law University, September 26, 2012.
25. Student papers, Texas A&M University, April 22, 2013.
26. Student papers, National Law University, October 28, 2013.
27. http://www.archive.org/stream/cu31924022240737/cu31924022240737_djvu.txt.
28. Student papers, Gujarat National Law University, September 26, 2012..
29. Student papers, National Law University, October 29, 2014.
30. http://www.bailii.org/uk/cases/UKHL/2003/61.html.
31. http://archive.org/stream/lawtortsatreati03pollgoog/lawortreati03pollgoog_djvu.txt.
32. http://scc.lexum.umontreal.ca/en/1989/1989rcs2-1181/1989rcs2-1181.pdf.
33. http://www.cila.co.uk/files/Adjustment%20of%20public%20Liability%20Claims.pdf.
34. Student papers, Gujarat National University, October 8, 2014.
35. http://www.legalservicesindia.com/articles/dct.htm.
36. Student papers, Gujarat National Law University, October 8, 2014.
37. http://www.drtssolutions.com/measure_of_damages.htm.
38. Student papers, National Law University, October 28, 2013.
39. Student papers, Gujarat National University, September 26, 2012.
40. http://society.ezinemark.com/general-defenses-in-tort-16ae390cfed.html.

41. http://www.indiankanoon.org/doc/657753.
42. Student papers, Gujarat National Law University, October 8, 2014.
43. http://www.legalcrystal.com/639674.
44. http://indiankanoon.org/doc/645953.
45. Student papers, Gujarat National Law University, September 26, 2012.
46. http://www.vakilno1.com/judgements/companiesact/1999-004clj0208sc.htm.
47. http://jklaws.in/details.aspx?id=48.
48. http://www.tndls.ac.in/pdf.
49. http://www.planet-diversity.org.
50. Student papers, National Law University, Orissa, August 13, 2013.
51. http://www.shabbirsite.yolasite.com/resources/Law of tort-john cooke.pdf.
52. http://www.lawteacher.net/Tort/Negligence/pdf.
53. Student papers, National Law University, New Delhi, October 29, 2014.
54. Student papers, National Law University, Orissa, August 13, 2013.
55. http://csa.org.in/SC2000Apr24.htm.
56. http://www.singaporelaw.sg/sglaw.
57. Student papers, O.P. Jindal Global University, March 26, 2012.
58. Student papers, O.P. Jindal Global University, April 16, 2012.
59. http://archive.org/stream/lawtortsatreati03pollgoog.
60. http://www.archive.org/stream/lawtortsatreati03pollgoog.
61. http://blog.legalbird.net/concept-of-strict-liability.html.
62. Student papers, Gujarat National Law University, May 29, 2012.
63. http://www.malaysianbar.org.
64. http://www.lawyersclubindia.com.
65. http://www.drtsolutions.com/measures-of-damages.htm.
66. http://www.lawtecher.net/tresspass-to-person.php.

67. Student papers, National Law University, New Delhi, October 29, 2014.
68. Student papers, Taylor's Education Group, October 16, 2014.
69. Student papers, Gujarat National Law University, September 26, 2012.
70. http://www.kamkus.org/pdf.
71. http://www.law.manchaster.ac.uk.
72. http://www.ngo-marg.org.
73. http://lassnet.org/2009/readings.pdf.
74. http://www.archive.org/stream.
75. http://www.audiocasefiles.com.
76. http://www.oup.com/uk/orc/bin/9780199268702/ch01.pdf.
77. Article 22 of the Constitution of India and Chapter V of CrPC, India.
78. http://www.lawnet.lk/docs/case-law/nlr/common/html/NLR16V73.htm.
79. http://www.intranet.holborncollege.ac.uk/tort.pdf.
80. Student papers, Wawasan Open University, February 21, 2011.
81. http://www.lawteacher.net/Negligence%20Breach%20cases.php.
82. Student papers, Athlone Institute of Technology, November 22, 2011.
83. Student papers, National Law School of India University, December 16, 2009.
84. http://www.jatingarg.in/uploads/5/7/0/6/5706755/contributory-and-composite-negligence.pdf.
85. http://www.contentcarry.com/all-india-bar-examination-abide-4-sample-question-paper/14951.
86. Student papers, Kenyatta University, April 8, 2014.
87. http://www.ipsofactoj.com/appeal/2003(2)-015.htm.
88. Student papers, University of Waikato, July 26, 2007.
89. http://www.fhrai.com/Mag-News/newsletlegal.asp.
90. Student papers, National Law University, New Delhi, October 30, 2014.

91. http://legalperspectives.blogspot.in.
92. Student papers, O.P. Jindal Global University, November 24, 2014.
93. http://www.tndls.ac.in/pdf/teaching material.
94. http://www.articeblast.com/Laws-and-Legal/General/Contributory-negligence-with-special-reference-to-moter-vehicle-accidents.
95. http://www.adhivaktaparishad.com/contributory-negligence.
96. Student papers, Christ College of Law, January 21, 2009.
97. Student papers, National Law University, New Delhi, May 23, 2014.
98. Student papers, Gujarat National Law University, May 15, 2013.
99. Student papers, Gujarat National Law University, September 26, 2012.
100. Student papers, National Law School of India University, Bangalore, December 16, 2009.

Annexures

Annexure 1

Important Facts about Torts

(Useful Points for Solving Objective Type Questions)

---

1. The word *tort* has been derived from the term *tortum* which is a Latin word.
2. The meaning of tort is twisted, crooked, unlawful, and not straight.
3. Tort is a breach of duty recognized under the law of torts.
4. Crime is a wrongful act which results from the breach of duty recognized by criminal law.
5. A breach of contract is the non-performance of a duty undertaken by a party to the contract.
6. In the case of civil wrong, the injured party is called plaintiff.
7. The wrong which are comparatively less serious are considered to be civil wrongs.
8. There are various wrongs which find their place both under criminal law and law of torts—assault, defamation, negligence, conspiracy, nuisance.
9. The criminal wrong is considered to be a public wrong.
10. Under a contract, parties themselves undertake certain obligations, fulfillment of which becomes a duty for both the parties. Where either party fails to fulfill its part of obligations, a breach of contract arises—damages are the main remedy, damages may be liquidated.
11. Damages in the case of tort are unliquidated.
12. In the case of breach of trust, the damages are liquidated.
13. The *Pigeon Hole theory* was propounded by Salmond.
14. Winfield's book is entitled Law of Tort.
15. 'Torts are infinitely various, not limited or confined'. This definition was given by C.J. Pratt.

16. To constitute a tort, the two essentials are actor omission and legal damage.
17. When there is a legal duty to do some act and a person fails to perform that he can be made liable for such omission.
18. Glouscester grammar school case explains the point *Damnum sine injuria*.
19. *Injuria* means infringement of a right.
20. *Damnum sine injuria* means a damage without the violation of legal right which is not actionable in a court of law.
21. In the cases of *injuria sine damnum,* it has to be proved that the plaintiff's legal right has been violated.
22. Mental state is an essential element in tortious liability.
23. Malice in law simply means wrongful intention.
24. The enactments which provide for compensation to the victim without going into the question of fault, include Fatal Accident Act, Workmen's Compensation Act and Motor Vehicle Act.
25. Liquidated damages—where the plaintiff in action sues for a pre-determined and inelastic sum of money, he is said to have claimed.
26. *Right in rem* means a right vested in some determinate person and available against the world at large.
27. *Right in personam* means a right available only against some determinate person or party.
28. Legal right means rights recognized by law and capable of being enforced by law courts.
29. If a person enters willingly into a sports event and receives grave injury, he has no claim in torts because of the principle of *volenti non fit injuria*.
30. For an action in tort, some legal rights should be damaged.
31. *Ashby vs. White* case is related to *injuria sine damnum*.
32. Law of torts is developed mainly through judicial decisions.
33. In Indian law, tort is defined as a civil wrong.

34. In English law, tort is defined as wrong.
35. In Roman law, tort is defined as delicit.
36. The reasons for the lack of tort litigation in India are: (a) undue delay in final disposal of cases, (b) high cost of litigation beyond the means of an average person, and (c) lack of consciousness about one's right and the spirit of toleration.
37. *Bhim Singh vs. State of J&K—Injuria sine damno.*
38. *Acton vs. Blundell—Damnum sine injuria.*
39. *Mogul steamship Co. vs. McGregor—Damnum sine injuria.*
40. *Ashby vs. White—Injuria sine damno.*
41. The meaning of the term *ubi remedium ibi jus* is where there is a remedy, there is a right.
42. The Common Law Procedure Act was passed in 1852.
43. If the same act, done by a person results in two wrongs—a crime as well as tort at the same time—in such a case, both civil and criminal remedy would be available.
44. More serious wrongs are considered to be public wrongs and are known as crimes.
45. If at any stage, the injured party likes, he may agree to a compromise with the tort feasor and withdraw the suit filed by him. This statement is about private wrong.
46. The term *Mens rea* is used for a guilty mind.
47. Salmond holds that there is no *law of tort* but there is *law of torts*.
48. Henry Maine observed that the penal law of primitive communities was not the law of crime but the law of wrongs and torts.
49. The element of malice is essential in torts of defamation, malicious prosecution, willful and malicious damage to property and maintenance and slander of life.
50. Malice in fact means wrongful act.
51. The maxim *salus populi supreme lex* means that the welfare of people is supreme law.
52. The term *Volenti non fit injuria* stands for consent.

53. Act of God is also known by the name *Vis major or Damnum Fatale.*
54. For the defence of act of God, there must be working of natural forces, the occurrence must be extraordinary and not one which could be anticipated and reasonably guarded against.
55. Rainfall, flood, storm, tide, volcano are all acts of God.
56. The essentials of an act of state are: (a) the act is done by the representative of the state, (b) the act is injurious to some other states or its subjects, (c) the act may be either previously sanctioned or subsequently ratified by the state.
57. When an agent commits a tort in the course of performance of his duty as an agent, the liability of the principal arises for such a wrongful act. In such a case, the plaintiff can sue both the agent and the principal.
58. The rule of absolute liability was first laid down by J. Blackburn in 1868.
59. *Qui facit per alium facit per se* establishes the vicarious liability.
60. If a wrong is committed by a servant, the liability of the master and servant is joint and several.
61. A servant is a person who voluntarily agrees to work under the control and command of another during the period of employment.
62. The tort of absolute liability is related to the escape of animal of a dangerous nature.
63. Under the doctrine of vicarious liability, principal is liable for the wrongful act of his agent, master is liable for the torts of his servant and partners are liable for each other's wrongful act.
64. A personal right of action ends with the person. This is about *Actio personalis moritur persone.*
65. The doctrine of the liability of master for the acts of servants is of modern growth. This is based on the maxim *respondeat superior.*

66. The rule of master's liability does not apply to the head of the department, as he is not liable for the wrongful act of his subordinates, for example, the post master general is not liable for the negligent act of a telegraph cable repairer.
67. If 'X' hires a taxi for going to railway station and the taxi driver 'Y' negligently hits 'Z', 'Y' will be liable.
68. Salmond defines *liability* as the bond of necessity that exists between the wrongdoer and the remedy of the wrong.
69. In a civil wrong, the liability is measured by wrongful act.
70. Two kinds of liability are civil and criminal. Penal liability is related with criminal liability.
71. Remedial liability is a civil liability, which is based on the maxim *Ubi jus ibi remedium.*
72. Two conditions of penal liability are act and guilty mind or *mensrea*.
73. A breach of the rule is called wrong.
74. After successful proceedings, a wrong doer is awarded: (a) fine, or (b) imprisonment or (c) punishment.
75. According to Austin, movement of the will is act.
76. Salmond defines act as the event which is subject to the control of human will.
77. The penal liability is only for voluntary acts.
78. External acts means the act of body.
79. Intentional act means the act which is foreseen and is desired by the doer.
80. The following are included in *mensrea*: (a) intention, (b) malice, (c) negligence, (d) needlessness, and (e) rashness.
81. The mistake of law is based on the maxim *Ignorantia juris non excusat.*
82. The general principle of law is that a person is liable for his own acts and not for the acts of others. But in certain types of cases, a person is made liable for the acts of others. This liability is called vicarious liability.

83. The representatives of the dead person are, in certain cases, liable for the acts of the deceased.
84. According to the English law, libel and slander are two important factors of defamation; libel is added to the eye, slander to the ear.
85. Under criminal law, libel has been recognized as an offence.
86. Both libel and slander are criminal offences under Section 499 of the I.P.C.
87. When there is imputation of unchastity to a woman by spoken words, the wrong is actionable.
88. In defamation, the term *innuendo* means the secondary meaning.
89. Essentials of defamation are: (a) the statement must be published, (b) the statement must be defamatory, (c) the said statement must refer to the plaintiff.
90. The essence of the defamation is injury to a person's character or reputation.
91. The defences to an action of defamation are: justification or truth; fair comment; privilege.
92. Libel is always actionable in tort.
93. Slander is actionable only on the proof of a special damage.
94. Slander is not an offence under criminal law.
95. Action lies for defamation in the following cases—written on the notice board; written in a telegram; written in a post card.
96. If, in a newspaper, there is publication of a statement of facts making serious allegations of dishonesty and corruption against the plaintiff: (a) The plea of fair comment can be taken if the defendant is able to prove the truth of such facts; (b) If the defendant is unable to prove the truth of such facts, the plea of fair comment will fail.
97. Following facts are considered to be the matters of public interest: the courts, public companies, public meetings and public institutions; conduct of public men like ministers,

officers of state; pictures, theatres, public entertainment, text books and novels.

98. No action for libel or slander lies against judges, counsels, witnesses.
99. Every unreasonable interference is nuisance.
100. If the interference is direct, the wrong is trespass.
101. Trespass is an interference with a person's possession of land.
102. When a person plants a tree over his own land and the roots or branches project onto or over the land of another person, that is a nuisance.
103. Nuisance can be committed through the medium of intangible objects.
104. Pollock defined nuisance as the wrong done to a man by unlawfully disturbing him in the enjoyment of his property, or, in some cases, in the exercise of some common rights.
105. Public nuisance is an offence punishable under criminal law.
106. In order to sustain a civil action in respect of a public nuisance, proof of special damage is essential; proof of damage is substantial.
107. If the plaintiff cannot prove that he has suffered any special damage, i.e. more damage than suffered by other members of the public, he can claim compensation.
108. To constitute a tort of nuisance, the following are required: unreasonable interference, interference with the use of enjoyment of land and damage.
109. If some noises, which do not disturb or annoy an ordinary person and disturb only the plaintiff in his work or sleep due to his over sensitiveness, there is no nuisance at all.
110. If a man creates nuisance or is acting unreasonably, he commits a legal wrong and is guilty of malicious wrong.
111. Right to property is not a natural right.
112. On the expiration of the period of 20 years, the nuisance becomes a legal right; an easement.

113. Writing, printing, picture, effigy, statute are not libel.
114. Section 1 of Defamation Act, 1952 provides that broadcasting of words by means of wireless telegraphy shall be treated as publication in permanent form.
115. Malicious prosecution consists of malicious criminal proceedings.
116. False accusation, malicious spirit, indirect or improper motive constitute malicious prosecution.
117. The plaintiff has to prove in a suit for damages for malicious prosecution: (a) that he was prosecuted by the defendant; (b) the prosecution was instituted without any reasonable and probable cause; (c) the defendant acted maliciously and not with the mere intention of carrying the law into effect; (d) plaintiff suffered damages as a result of the prosecution.
118. Prosecution means criminal proceedings; a criminal charge made before a judicial officer.
119. A proceeding before police authorities is no prosecution.
120. Fees paid to the counsel or *vakil* in defending the accused person in prosecution can also be allowed as damages.
121. In a case of malicious prosecution, the court considers: (a) the nature of the offence which the plaintiff was charged of; (b) the inconvenience to which the plaintiff was subjected to; (c) monetary loss; (d) the status and position of the person.
122. When the legal process is abused, it results in a tort.
123. An essential element of false imprisonment—total restraint on the liberty of a person; it should be without any lawful justification.
124. Wrongful restraint and wrongful confinement are described under Sections 339 and 340 of the I.P.C.
125. Tort of false imprisonment is complete when restraint is total.
126. Knowledge of the plaintiff that there has been restraint on his freedom is necessary.

127. The difference between malicious prosecution and false imprisonment is that in malicious prosecution, the imprisonment is proved by a judgement or judicial order.
128. In tort, the action is brought by the injured party.
129. An absolute remedy for the torts is an action for damages.
130. Right in rem is available against the world.
131. Legal damage is neither identical with an actual damage nor is necessarily pecuniary.
132. Justenian defines *injury* as every action contrary to law.
133. In malicious, the actual damage is not the gist of action.
134. All persons who aid or counsel or direct or join in the committal of a wrongful act are joint tort feasors.
135. Smoke constitutes private nuisance.
136. Obstruction to light and air constitutes private nuisance.
137. Interference with electricity constitutes private nuisance.
138. Interference with disease producing germs constitutes private nuisance.
139. Interference with vegetation constitutes private nuisance.
140. Interference with trees constitutes private nuisance.
141. Interference with animals constitutes private nuisance.
142. Plaintiff must prove that the prosecution was instituted against him without any reasonable or probable cause.
143. In an action for malicious prosecution, the plaintiff must prove that the prosecution was instituted with a malicious intention.
144. A person can be imprisoned while he is insane.
145. Wrongful arrest by a private person or by a public officer will constitute false imprisonment.
146. If it is made by legal warrant executed at an unlawful time, the arrest is unlawful.
147. The period for which detention continues in case of false imprisonment is material.
148. If arrest is made without warrant, it is wrongful.
149. English laws of maintenance and champerty are not in force as specific laws in India.
150. Negligence has been considered as an independent tort.

151. Negligence has two meanings in law of torts.
152. Negligence means a conduct, which creates a risk of causing damage rather than a state of mind.
153. In an action for negligence, the plaintiff has to prove that the defendant made a breach of that duty.
154. Lord Macmillan stated, "The categories of negligence are never closed".
155. Lord Atkin defined neighbors as "persons so closely and directly affected by my act that I ought reasonably to have them in contemplation as being so affected when I am directing my mind to act or omissions which are called in questions".
156. The standard of the foresight of a reasonable man is in one sense an impersonal act.
157. 'A' slipped into a pit filled with rainwater. He caught hold of a nearby electric pole to avert a fall. Due to leakage in electricity in the pole, he was electrocuted and died. The person who maintained the electric pole would be held liable.
158. A medical practitioner, when consulted by a patient, owes him a duty of care in deciding whether to undertake to case; a duty of care in deciding what treatment to give; a duty of care in the administration of the treatment.
159. The objective theory of the nature and definition of negligence says that the negligence is a type of conduct.
160. *Res Ipsa loquitur* maxim implies rule of evidence.
161. *Res ipsa loquitur* maxim shifts the burden of proving negligence on defendant.
162. *Res ipsa loquitur* means that the thing speaks for itself.
163. Ingredient of negligence—the duty was towards the plaintiff; defendant was under a legal duty; there was breach of duty.
164. "Negligence is culpable carelessness", this viewpoint was expressed by Austin.
165. *Res ipsa loquitur* is a defence of some factor which was beyond the control of person who caused injury.

166. In contributory negligence, both parties have contributed to negligence.
167. If 'P' gives lift in his car to 'Q' up to a certain place and on the way due to the negligence of 'P', an accident is caused, 'P' has a legal duty to take care of 'Q' and is also liable for compensation.
168. Austin stated that "negligence is a faulty mental condition which is penalized by award of damage".
169. To be guilty of contributory negligence, the person should have acted like a prudent man.
170. The last opportunity rule is related with contributory negligence.
171. On the part of children, the case of contributory negligence cannot be registered.
172. When the negligence of two or more persons results in the same damage, there is said to be composite negligence.
173. In a case of composite negligence, the liability of composite tort feasors is joint and several.
174. When two or more persons commit same tort against the same plaintiff, they may be joint tort feasors.
175. Strict liability arises if some dangerous things have been brought by a person on his land; if the thing thus brought or kept by a person on his land must escape if it is non-natural use of land.
176. When two or more persons without lawful justification combine for the purpose of willfully causing damage to the plaintiff and the actual damage results there from, they commit the tort of conspiracy.
177. Tort is a violation of a right in rem.
178. No action lies against a witness for what he says or writes by giving evidence before a court of justice.
179. The law of tort is largely uncodified.
180. Some other subjects of law in tort are: The Workmen's Compensation Act, 1923; The Specific Relief Act, 1963; Employer's Liability Act; Easement Act, 1882.
181. Assault and nuisance are wrongs under tort.

182. Pointing a loaded pistol at another is an assault.
183. In India, English law is adopted except where found unsuitable to local conditions in India.
184. Unliquidated damage means damage to be assessed by the court as these are not pre-determined.
185. Wrongs affecting safety and freedom of a person: assault, battery, false imprisonment.
186. Malicious prosecution is known as the abuse of legal procedure.
187. The liability for the damage done by animals can be studied under Scienter Rule; cattle trespass; ordinary liability in tort.
188. According to the Scienter Rule, the animals have been divided into two categories—animals dangerous by nature and animals harmless by nature.
189. According to the Scienter Rule, the dangerous animals include lions, tigers, elephants, monkeys.
190. A person who keeps animals with the knowledge of its tendency to harm is strictly liable for damage.
191. Lions, tigers, bears, elephants and monkeys have been considered to be generally dangerous to mankind and are therefore, placed in the category of fearer nature.
192. If a monkey kept by the defendant bites the plaintiff, the defendant will be liable without the proof of negligence.
193. The Dogs Act, 1906 makes the liability of the owner of the dog strict in certain cases. He is liable: (a) for injury done to cattle by the dog without the proof of dog's mischievous propensity; (b) for injury done to poultry by the dog without the proof of dog's mischievous propensity.
194. Keeping dogs in some premises which causes unreasonable interference with the neighbour's enjoyment of his property is a nuisance.
195. If a person plants a tree over his land and its roots or branches escape onto the land of neighbour that will be a nuisance.

196. Where a person is injured without any negligence on his part but as a result of the combined effect of the negligence of two persons, it is a case of composite negligence.
197. In negligence, breach of duty means non-observance of due care.
198. In the case of death of a person in a motor vehicle accident, liability would arise both with or without fault.
199. A public wrong means a wrong done to whole community.
200. Two motorists driving negligently and coming from the opposite direction collide and a pedestrian is crushed between the two cars, the motorists are independent tort feasors.
201. 'A' and 'B' entered 'Z's premises to search for an escape of gas, each one of them and in turn, applied naked light to the gas pipe. A's application resulted in an explosion causing damage to Z's premises. 'A' and 'B' both are liable.
202. A wife can sue her husband if the husband damaged her watch.
203. If a wife committed a tort, there could be an action under the Married Women's Property Act, 1882 against both wife and husband.
204. If a magistrate is acting maliciously, corruptly or without a reasonable or probable cause in law, it is called malafide.
205. The meaning of the maxim *respondent superior* is let the principal be liable.
206. An independent contractor is not subject to the control and supervision of his employer.
207. An independent contractor is one who undertakes to do certain works and regarding the manner in which the work is to be done.

208. Tort committed while performing duty in discharge of obligations imposed by law has been considered to be a defence in India.
209. The protection of judicial privilege is available only if the officer is acting judicially.
210. Whenever the plaintiff has been wrongfully detained, he can always bring action of *habeas corpus*, self-help, damages.
211. The rule of strict liability was formulated by the House of Lords in *Rylands vs. Fletcher* case in 1868.
212. The strict liability is also known as no fault liability.
213. If there is negligence on the part of the manufacturer or seller of goods and the buyers suffers thereby, he can sue the manufacturer and the seller under law of tort.
214. Most parts of the law of torts grew out of writs.
215. Assault and nuisance are wrongs under criminal law and tort.
216. The meaning of the maxim *Ubi jus ibi remedium* is where there is right, there is remedy.
217. In law of torts, the remedies available are: (a) damages, (b) injunctions, (c) specific restitution.
218. When a person's normal span of life is shortened due to the negligence of the defendant, the right to claim compensation devolves on the legal representative and they can claim compensation on behalf of the deceased.
219. The case of *Kasturilal vs. State of U.P.* related to state liability in law of tort.
220. In the case of *Priestley vs. Flower*—the doctrine of *common employment* was first laid down.
221. The rule, burden to prove that he was not negligent lies on the defendant, is expressed by the phrase *res ipsa loquiter*.
222. *Reasonable foresight* as a test to determine remoteness of consequences was laid down in The Wagon Mound case.
223. In tort, act of the third party is a defence in strict liability.

224. A tort is a civil wrong for which the remedy is a civil action for unliquidated damages.
225. *Ashby vs. White*—a case related with *Injuria sine damno.*
226. Corporation is a legal person.
227. In vicarious liability, the master is liable only when the servant's wrong falls within the course of his employment.
228. For a defence of the consent to succeed, it is necessary for the defendant to establish that the plaintiff knew of the risk and therefore impliedly assented to it.
229. A claim under the (Indian) Fatal Accidents Act, 1855, can be made only on behalf of certain heirs, i.e., the wife, husband, parent or child. No action can be brought by the brothers and sisters of the deceased.

Annexure 2

Important Questions for UPSC and Other PCS Examinations

---

1. When can a defendant plead 'voluntary assumption of risk' by the plaintiff as a ground of defence in an action in tort?
2. What are the conditions of application of the maxim *res ipsa loquitur?* How does it affect the burden of proof in cases of negligence?
3. "The maxim *res ipsa loquitor* is not a rule of law but a rule of evidence." Explain.
4. Study very carefully the following two situations:
- **Situation A:** While playing on a cricket ground owned by the defendant, a batsman hits the ball so hard that it went over the boundary wall and hit the plaintiff walking on an adjoining street. In the history of the eighty year old ground, the ball had been so hit out 5 or 6 times.
- **Situation B:** Trespassing children used to play football in an open area belonging to the defendant adjoining a busy road. In the absence of a high boundary wall, the ball used to go on the road frequently and children used to go there to fetch the ball back. One day the ball was shot out on the road where it hit a scooter driver causing him to fall and suffer injuries.

   Compare the tortuous liability of the defendants in above mentioned situations. Give reasons and cite case law.
5. Employees of the telecommunication department opened a manhole in a street near a children's park and in the evening left the open manhole covered by a canvas tent unattended and surrounded by warning paraffin lamps. The plaintiff, a boy aged 8, attracted by the lamps and the tent, entered into the tent. While peeping into the manhole

he stumbled over the lamp. The lamp fell into the manhole and in a violent explosion that followed the plaintiff sustained burn injuries. In an action in tort, the dependant pleads remoteness of damage. Decide.

6. What is meant by *innuendo*? What are the facts which the plaintiff must prove or establish in order to sustain a plea of innuendo?
7. A journalist, writes an article against B, a public servant, alleging that B has misappropriated a sum of ₹ 2 lakh from the public fund under his control. In an action in tort for defamation by B against him, A takes the defence of fair comment. Discuss with reasons.
8. "A wrong falls within the course of employment of the servant if it is necessarily incidental to something which servant is employed to do". Explain.
9. Explain the elements of the tort of private nuisance.
10. "Under the tort of nuisance a person cannot increase the liabilities of his neighbour by applying his own property to special uses, whether for business or pleasure". Examine.
11. A, the owner of a house, allows the branches of a tree in his compound to overhang the adjoining highway. B, a driver of the city bus corporation, drives a bus negligently very close to the overhanging branches such that the branches injure a passenger in the bus through a window, and loses his eyes. From whom can the passenger recover damages to the loss of the amenity, from B, the city bus corporation, or A, or from all the three?
12. Study very carefully the following two situations:

- **Situation A:** The defendant, a deeply religious man and owner of a house in the heart of the city, set it apart free for rent to those who wished to use the same for religious purposes. As a result, the house remained occupied most of the time. The music played through the loudspeaker during religious ceremonies caused constant noise and inconvenience to the neighbours.

- **Situation B:** The defendant established a flour mill in a residential area in the heart of the city adjacent to the plaintiff's house. Continuous running of the mill for long hours every day caused unpleasant noise as well as continuous vibrations in the house of the plaintiff.

  Compare the tortuous liability of the defendants in the above mentioned situations. Give reasons and cite case law.

13. "In tort, the plaintiff wins his case only when he proves as to what particular tort the defendant has committed against him". Examine.
14. "Law of tort is based upon a fundamental general principle that it is wrongful to cause harm to other persons in the absence of some specific ground of justification or excuse". Examine.
15. On what grounds can a person committing any harm on a consenting individual be not punished? Is there any limit to the harm or can it be the harm to any extent?
16. "Duties in tort exist by the virtue of the law itself, and are not dependant upon the consent of the persons subjected to them". Examine.
17. A question based on the facts of *Cassidy vs. Daily Mirror Newspaper Ltd.* case.
18. Distinguish the wrong committed in the following:

- A solicitor, acting on behalf of his client, dictated a letter to the plaintiff stating therein that she (plaintiff) bears an immoral character. The letter then was posted to the plaintiff.
- X told Z that Y is suffering from AIDS though the statement is not true.

19. Discuss the legal principles, in the background of the recent changes in the law, applicable to the determination of liability for injury caused by "hazardous substances" and also the nature of the said liability.
20. "The mere fact that a process or business is useful to persons generally. In spite of its annoyance to the plaintiff,

is there no defence to an action for the tort of nuisance". Examine.

21. Explain the common law doctrine of contributory negligence and the illogicality involved in it that paves the way for its modification.
22. Distinguish the wrong committed in the following:

- The defendant told the plaintiff to leave the premises in occupation of the plaintiff. When the plaintiff refused, the defendant collected some of his workmen who mustered round the plaintiff, tucking up their sleeves and aprons and threatened to break the plaintiff's neck if he did not leave. The plaintiff then left the place.
- A takes B by the collar and pushes him down the hill.

23. How do you distinguish between wrongful imprisonment and wrongful restraint? Explain with illustration.
24. Examine the tortious liability of A in the following: A pretends to lock the plaintiff in a room by purporting to turn the key of the door from outside and taking it away. The fact is that the door, though shot, is not locked. The plaintiff remains in the room for two hours under the belief that he has been locked inside.
25. "'If I snatch your hat from your head and throw it at any other person that is trespass to your hat, but it is not conversion, for I am not questioning your title to it. But if I take it from you with intent to steal it, that is conversion as well as trespass'" (Winfield).

    X receives from B, a bookseller, a parcel of books, which X did not order. X wrote to B to arrange for taking them back soon as he did not want to buy them. After three months, X received a letter from B asking X to hand them over to a local book dealer. By this time the books became moth-eaten and unfit for sale. Can B sue X for conversion and recover the price of the book?
26. "In the law of tort for malicious prosecution, the plaintiff must prove, among other things, that the defendant was the

person who was actively instrumental in putting the law in force". Examine.

27. Examine the statement that what is lawful if one may become unlawful and when done by more than one acting in combination.
28. "The purpose of a combination and the means employed to achieve that purpose are the two most important considerations in the tort of conspiracy".
29. "The fact must support the implication from occupier's conduct that he has permitted entry, not merely tolerated it, for knowledge is not tantamount to consent". Discuss with reference to the liability of the occupier towards a licensee. Is it in any way different towards a trespasser explain
30. A person was running a saw mill. He allowed young boys in the locality to come and watch the working of the machine from a distance. One day unnoticed bў anyone, a young boy of eight years went very near the machine and put his hand in it. The hand was severed. The boy represented by his father instituted a suit for damages. Will he succeed?
31. What is the liability, if any, for negligent misstatement which causes financial loss to the plaintiff?
32. 'The basic principle for the measure of damages in tort as well as in contract is that there should be *restitutio in integram'*. Explain and comment.
33. When do the courts award exemplary damages in an action for tort?
34. Examine the tortuous liability of A in the following situation:
    Branches of a tree grown on B's land overhang in the side of A, his neighbour. A repeatedly requests B to cut off these branches so that A is able to enjoy sunlight. B does not pay heed to these requests. A goes on to the side of B and cuts off those branches.
35. Critically examine the concept of "tortious liability" as defined by Winfield. Distinguish between tort and crime.

36. A asks for a lift from a motorist D. D told A, "I am not an expert driver. I am without a driving licence too. You may travel at your own risk". A travels with D. Later, the motor vehicle collided with a bus due to defective brakes of D's vehicle. A sues D for injuries suffered by him in the accident. D pleaded *volenti non fit injuria.* Decide.
37. BPL Sanyo, a company, erected huge hoarding displaying their products at a road trisection. On a windy day, the hoarding fell down and seriously injured a cyclist going alongside the road. He has no proof of negligence. Will he succeed in action against the company? Decide.
38. What do you understand by remoteness of damage? What is the true test of remoteness?
39. "The test of forseeability in preference to the test of directness has now become established by the Wagon Mound case". Discuss.
40. Whether the test of foreseeability could be applied to a tort of nuisance or a tort of strict liability?
41. Examine the differences between the rule in *Ryland vs. Fletcher* and the rule in *M.C. Mehta vs. Union of India.* Which rule will you advocate in the present day Indian society?
42. Discuss the law relating to the vicarious liability of the Government of India. Do you think the present law is not satisfactory?

    P, a police constable, searched the person of A, on his arrest, and seized a sum of ₹ 5,000 believing the money to be stolen property. Can A sue the Government for the recovery of the amount?
43. Critically examine the vicarious liability of the state under Article 300 of the Constitution of India?
44. A gatekeeper at a rail crossing negligently allowed the gate to remain open and therein impliedly invited people to cross the railway line. M and his wife W, who were driving in a buggy, entered the gate at the crossing with reasonable care on their part but without realizing that a

train was approaching fast. Luckily there was no collision with the train, but the escape was so narrow and the danger so alarming that W fainted and suffered a severe nervous shock which produced prolonged illness. X, who had already crossed the level crossing on foot, saw the hair-breadth's escape of W and M, and also suffered a nervous shock resulting in illness. Decide.

45. Discuss whether the damage is a foreseeable consequence or is too remote in the following cases:

- Damage resulting from judicial act.
- Damage resulting from the wrongful act of the defendant aggravated by unusual sensitiveness of the plaintiff.
- A sterilization operation negligently performed by the doctors resulting in the plaintiff becoming pregnant. She decided not to have abortion and later gave birth to a child which was congenitally abnormal.
- A's car is damaged because of the B's negligence and it is taken to a garage for repairs wherefrom it is stolen.

46. "No defendant can be held liable *ad infinitum* for all the consequences which follow his wrongful acts. He is held liable only for those consequences which are not too remote". Do you agree with this observation? Discuss with reference to the tests to determine the remoteness of the damages.

47. A notorious criminal murdered several persons in the city of Delhi. The Delhi Police failed to identify and apprehend him. The criminal killed another person, M. The parents of M sued Delhi Police for its breach of duty towards the member of the public. Will they succeed in their action? Decide.

48. On one winter morning, while the weather was very foggy and visibility was very poor, M drove from Shakti Nagar to Dhaula Kuan and on his way had an accident with L, who was killed as a consequence. L's heir filed a case against M seeking damages. M pleaded Act of God as a

defence. Discuss the liability of M by stating the extent and scope of the defence.

49. Although a tort is a civil injury, not all civil injuries are torts, for no civil injury is to be classed as a tort unless the appropriate remedy for it is an action for unliquidated damages. Comment and discuss the elements of tort.
50. What is tort? Discuss the definitions given by various jurists and critically examine/appreciate the same.

Annexure 3

Model Questions and Answers

Question: "It is far too sweeping proposition to say that when it has been once determined that there is evidence of negligence, the person guilty of it is equally liable for it whether he could have foreseen it or not", Comment.

Answer: The issue under consideration in the present case is the law relating to the remoteness of damage in the law of tort.

As a general statement, it may be noted that consequences of a wrongful act are infinite, but in law of tort, the defendant is liable for those consequences which are not too 'remote' from his conduct. The word remote is used as an antonym to proximate. Conversely stated, whatever is not the direct and immediate result of the wrongful act is a remote consequence.

In the course of judicial evolution of the concept of remoteness of damage, two main tests emerged:

1. The test of reasonable foresight.
2. The test of directness.

The test of reasonable foresight emerged from the dicta of Pollock, C.B. in *Rigby vs. Hewit*, 1850, 5 Ex 240 and *Greenland vs. Chaplin*, 1850, 5 Ex 243, wherein it was held that the liability of the defendant is only for those consequences which could have been foreseen by a reasonable man placed in the circumstances of the wrongdoer.

The test of reasonable foresight was acceptable to the judiciary till 1921, when Scrutton, L.J., rejected it and propounded the test of directness in re: Polemis and Furness Withy & Co. Ltd. (1921) 3Kb 560. In this case, a ship carried a quantity of petrol in tins. Due to leakage in those tins, some of their contents collected in the hold of the shop. Owing to the negligence of the defendant's servants, a plank fell into the hold and a spark was caused and consequently the ship was totally destroyed by fire. The owners of the ship were held entitled to recoveries, it being the direct consequence of the wrongful act although such a loss could not have been reasonably foreseen. According to Scrutton, L.J., "To determine whether an act is negligent it is relevant whether any reasonable person would foresee that the act would cause damage: if he would not, act is not negligent. But if the act would or might probably cause damage, the fact that the damage in fact caused is in not the exact kind of damage one would expect, is immaterial so long as the damage is in fact directly traceable to the negligent act...".

This test was previously applied in the case of *Smith vs. London and South Western Railway Company*, 1870, LR6 Cr 14, where a railway company negligently allowed a heap of trimmings of hedges and grass to lie near a railway line. A spark from the railway engine set fire to the material, which due to high wind was carried to the plaintiff's cottage which was burnt. The defendants were held liable even though they could not have foreseen the loss to the cottage.

The scope of the above test was limited by the House of Lords in *Liesbosch Dredger vs. Edison*, 1933, AC 449. In this case, owing to the negligence of the defendant, the dredger Liesbosch was sunk. The owners of Liesboch required it for the performance of a contract with a third party, but since they were too poor to purchase a new one, they hired one at an exorbitant rate. They sued the defendants for compensation, inter alia, for the hire charges which they had to pay from the date of the sinking to the date they could actually purchase a new dredger. The House of Lords allowed damages only till the date when another dredger could reasonably have been put to work. The claim after that time was rejected. The reason why new dredger could not be purchased by the plaintiffs was their poverty and it was considered an extraneous cause and as such too remote.

The test of directness has been considered to be incorrect by the Privy Council in *Overseas Tankship (U.K.) Ltd. vs. Morts Dock and Engineering Co. Ltd.* (Wagon Mound NO.1 case), 1961, 1 All ER 404 (PC) and it was held that the test of reasonable foresight is the better test. In this case, the wagon Mound, as an oil burning vessel, was chartered by the applicants and was taking fuel oil at the Sydney port. At a distance of about 600 feet, the respondents, Morts Dock Company, owned a wharf, where some welding operations were going on. Due to the negligence of the appellants' servants, a large quantity of oil was spilt on the water and carried to the respondent's wharf. Molten metal from the respondent's wharf fell on it and the resultant fire caused great damage to the wharf and the equipment. It was established that such damage could not have been reasonably foreseen. Wiscount Simons L.J., held, "...a man must be considered to be responsible for the probable consequences of his act.

The civilised order requires the observance of a minimum standard of behaviour...and since a reasonable man could not foresee such an injury, the appellants were not liable even though their act was the direct cause of the damage".

This ruling was approved by the House of Lords in *Hughes vs. Lord Advocate*, 1993, 1 All ER 705 (HL). In this case, the post office employees' who had opened a manhole for the purpose of maintaining underground telephone equipment, left it open and unguarded though surrounded by paraffin lamps. A child started playing with one of the lamps, which fell into the manhole and caused a violent explosion resulting in the fall of the boy also in the hole and causing severe injuries to him. It was foreseeable that a child could get burnt by playing with the lamp, but the explosion could not be foreseen. The House of Lords held that since the kind of damage was foreseeable although the extent was not, the defendants were liable.

Another case in which the test of reasonable foresight has been applied was in *Doughty vs. Turner Manufacturing Co.*

Ltd., 1964, 1 All ER 98 (CA). In this case, servants of the defendant let an asbestos cement cover to slope into a cauldron of hot molten liquid. It resulted in an explosion causing injuries to the plaintiff, who was standing nearby. It was established that nobody could foresee that an explosion could follow by the falling of the asbestos cover into the cauldron. It was held, that the damage resulting from the explosion was not of the kind as could have been reasonably foreseen, the defendants were held not liable The test has also been applied in *S.C.M. (United Kingdom) Ltd. vs. W.J. Whittal & Sone*, 1991, 1 QB 337, where due to the negligence of the defendant's workmen, an electric cable was damaged. As a result, there was a seven hour power failure in the plaintiff's factory. The plaintiff claimed compensation for damage to materials and machines and consequent loss of production. It was held that the defendants knew that the said electric cables supplied electric current to the factories and that they could foresee the loss of production, due to power failure, therefore, they were liable for the damage

Hence, forseeability has become as accepted test for determination of damages, and directness has been rejected.

Question: Explain the legal principle which is applied by the courts to decide whether a legal duty to take care exists in a given case or not.

'P' boarded an overcrowded red line bus at the authorized bus stop. Just when he had placed his foot on the foot board of the bus and had not yet gone in, the conductor in a very great haste rang the bell and the driver started the bus. The driver made an attempt to overtake another stationary bus so closely that 'P' got squeezed between the two buses and sustained serious injuries. P files a suit against the driver and conductor of the bus for claiming damages suffered by him on account of injuries. Decide.

Answer: The issue under consideration in the present case is the law relating to negligence.

Negligence means neglect to take care. It is the omission to do something which a reasonable man guided upon those considerations which ordinarily regulate the conduct of human affairs, would do or doing something which a prudent and reasonable man would not do. Or as stated in *Heaven vs. Pender*, 1883, 11 QBD 503, "actionable negligence consists in the neglect to the use of ordinary care of skill towards a person to whom the defendant owes the duty of observing ordinary care and skill, by which neglect, the plaintiff has suffered injury, to person or property".

There are three essential ingredients of negligence in the law of torts:

1. That the defendant owed duty of care to the plaintiff.
2. That the defendant made a breach of that duty.
3. That the plaintiff suffered damage as a consequence.

'Duty of care' means a legal duty. As to it, Lord Atkin propounded the following rule in *Donoghue vs. Stevenson*, 1932, Ac 562 (HL).

"The rule that you are to love your neighbour, becomes in law that you must not injure your neighbour. Who is my neighbour? You must take reasonable care to avoid acts or omissions which you can reasonably foresee would be likely to injure your neighbours. Who then is my neighbour? Persons so closely and directly affected by my act that I ought reasonably to have them in contemplation as being so affected when I direct my mind to the acts or omissions which are called in question.

It is evident from the test laid down by Lord Atkin that duty depends on the reasonable foreseeability of injury. Lord Macmillan observed in *Glasgow Corporation vs. Muir*, 1943 AC 447, "The standard of foresight of the reasonable man is in one sense an impersonal test...The reasonable man is presumed to be free both from over apprehension and from over-confidence".

Thus, in *Rural Transport Service vs. Bezlum Bibi*, AIR, 1980, Cal 165, the conductor of an over loaded bus invited passengers to travel on the roof of the bus. One of the passengers on the roof of the bus was struck by an overhanging branch of a tree and as a consequence thereof died. It was held that there was negligence on the part of both the driver and the conductor of the bus, and the defendants were liable for "inviting passengers to travel precariously on the top of an overcrowded bus which in itself is a rash and negligent act".

It is also negligence to start a bus before passengers get into it, as was decided in *Ishwar Devi vs. Union of India*, AIR, 1969, Del 183, where just as the deceased had placed his foot on the footboard of the bus and had not yet gone in, the conductor rang the bell and the driver started the bus. The driver made an attempt to overtake another stationary bus so closely that the deceased got squeezed between the two buses. It was held that both the driver and the conductor were rash and negligent in not taking proper care of the safety of the passengers.

In another case of negligence by Public Road Transport employees, *Sushma Mitra vs. Madhya Pradesh State Road Transport Corporation*, 1974, ACJ 87 (MP), the plaintiff was resting her elbow in the window sill. A truck coming from the opposite direction hit her in her elbow as a result of which she received severe injuries. It was held that the habit of resting elbow in the window of the bus is so common that it must enter into contemplation of a reasonable driver. It is the duty of the driver to pass on the road at a reasonable distance from the other vehicle so as to avoid any injury to the passengers whose limbs might be protruding beyond the body of the vehicle in the ordinary course.

The converse proposition that there is no liability when injury is not foreseeable is illustrated by the case of *Glasgow Corporation vs. Muir,* 1943, AC 447, where the manageress of tea rooms permitted a picnic party to have their food in the tea room. Two members of the picnic party were carrying a big urn containing six to nine gallons of tea to the tea room through a passage where there were some children. Suddenly one of the persons lost the grip of the handle of the urn and six children including the plaintiff were injured. It was held that the manageress could not anticipate that such an event would happen as a consequence of tea urn being carried through the passage and therefore, she had no duty to take precautions against the occurrence of such an event.

The following cases also illustrate the proposition that reasonable foreseeability does not mean remote possibility. The duty is to guard against probabilities rather than bare possibilities. Thus, in *Fardon vs. Harcourt-Rivington,* 1932, 146 LT 391, the defendant left a dog inside his parked car. The dog smashed a glass panel, which injured the plaintiff. It was held that the accident being very unlikely there was no negligence in not taking a precaution against it...People must guard against reasonable probabilities but they are not bound to guard against fantastic possibilities.

In *Blyth vs. Birmingham Waterworks Co.,* 1856, 11 Ex 781, due to exceptionally severe frost, a water plug installed by the defendants was damaged and as a result the plaintiff's premises were flooded. It was held that the defendants had provided against such frosts, as experience would have led man, acting prudently, against; and they were not guilty of negligence, because their precautions proved insufficient against the effect of the extreme severity of the frost of 1855, which penetrated to a greater depth than any which ordinarily occurs south of the polar regions.

Though obvious, it needs to be emphasized that mere carelessness on the part of the defendant does not entitle the plaintiff to sue him, for it has to be proved that the defendant owed a duty of care to the plaintiff. Thus in *Bourhill vs. Young*, 1943, AC 92 (HL), a fishwife had just alighted from a tramcar. A speeding motor cyclist passed on the other side of the tramcar and immediately afterwards collided with a motor car and was killed. The fishwife did not see the motor cyclist or the accident which had occurred but she simply heard the noise of the collision. In consequence, she sustained nervous shock. In her suit for damages, it was held by Lord MacMillan that the cyclist was under no duty to the appellant to foresee that his negligence in driving at an excessive speed and consequently colliding with a motor car might result in an injury to her, for such a result could not reasonably and probably be anticipated.

As to the standard of care required, it varies according to each situation. The kind of risk determines the precautions which defendant is expected to take. Thus, in *Glasgow Corporation vs. Muir*, 1943, A C447, poisonous berries in the defendants land looked like cherries and thus had tempting appearance for the children. A child, aged seven, ate those berries and died. It was held that the defendants were liable for negligence as they ought to have anticipated this possibility and taken appropriate precautions.

Decision to the Case in Question: The driver and the conductor of the bus owed a duty of care to 'P', and they were both rash and negligent in starting and overtaking when a passenger had not fully boarded the bus. The defendants are, therefore, liable for damages. A case in support is *Ishwar Devi vs. Union of India*, AIR, 1969, Del 183.

Annexure 4

Format of Writ Petition

A. Synopsis and list of dates (Specimen enclosed)

B. From next page...In the Supreme Court of India, Original Jurisdiction Civil Writ Petition No. of 2015. In the Matter of

...........Petitioner

Versus

..........Respondents

Petition under Article................of the Constitution of India for issuance of a writ in the nature of.........under Article............of the Constitution of India.

To,

The Hon'ble Chief Justice of India and His Lordship's Companion Justices of the Supreme Court of India. The humble petition of the petitioner above named.

Most respectfully sheweth:

1. Facts of the case
2. Question(s) of Law
3. Grounds
4. Averment:

   That the present petitioner has not filed any other petition in any High Court or the Supreme Court of India on the subject matter of the present petition.

Prayer

In the above premises, it is prayed that this Hon'ble Court may be pleased:

(I) ....

(II) to pass such other orders and further orders as may be deemed necessary on the facts and in the circumstances of the case.

For which act of kindness, the petitioner shall as in duty bound, ever pray.

Filed by:
Petitioner-in-person
Drawn:
Filed on:

....

C. The writ petition should be accompanied by:

1. Affidavit of the petitioner duly sworn.
2. Annexure as referred to in the writ petition; ₹ 2 per annexure.
3. 1+5 copies of the writ petition are required.
4. Court fee of ₹ 50 per petitioner (in criminal matter, no court fee is payable).
5. Index (as per specimen enclosed).
6. Cover page (as per specimen enclosed).
7. Any application to be filed; ₹ 12 per application.
8. Memo of appearance, ₹ 5 court fee.

Petitioner-in-person may see a copy of WP (kept with AR-IB) to have practical knowledge about drafting of petition.

Index

S. No.	Particulars	Pages
1.	Synopsis and list of dates.	
2.	Writ petition along with affidavit in support.	
3.	Annexure.	
4.	Application, if any.	

In the Supreme Court of India
Original Jurisdiction

Civil Writ Petition No……of 2015

………Petitioner

Versus

………Respondent

Paper Book

For index kindly see inside

Filed by:
(Advocate for the petitioner/petitioner-in-person)

Filed on:
Reference: www.supremecourtofindia.nic.in

Annexure 5

Specimen Form of a Writ Petition

In the High Court of........................at...................

Civil Original (Extra-ordinary) Jurisdiction

Civil Writ Petition No...........of 2015

In the matter of:
JKL S/o..............R/o..........former employee (Inspector Grade-I) in the respondent company.

......Petitioner

1. XYZ Company Ltd., a company wholly owned by the Government of India and having its registered office at........through its chairman.
2. Managing Director of the above company

.......Respondent

Civil Writ Petition against the order dated....... passed by the Managing Director, respondent no. 2 herein, by which the services of the petitioner as an employee of the respondent-company have been terminated.

May it please the Hon'ble Chief Justice of the High Court of ...... and His Lordship's Companion Judges.

The Petitioner
Most Respectfully Showeth:

1. That the petitioner is a citizen of India and is therefore entitled to enjoy all the rights guaranteed by the Constitution of India.

2. That respondent no. 1 is a company registered under the Companies Act, 1956 having its registered office at ....The respondent company is wholly owned by the Government of India and is, thus, an instrumentality of state as given in Annexure 12 of the Constitution.
3. That the petitioner was an employee of the respondent company, having been appointed as a Sub-Inspector Grade-I on..........1991and he continued to work, earning one promotion also.
4. That on ....20........respondent no. 2 herein abruptly issued the impugned order dated..........terminating the service of the petitioner and the petitioner came to be relieved of his duties the same day. A copy of the impugned order is annexed hereto and marked as Annexure 1.
5. That on a bare reading of the impugned order it becomes clear that the order has been issued on the basis of some alleged misconduct on the part of petitioner, but no inquiry under the relevant rules has been held before the passing of the order.
6. That the petitioner has not committed any act that could be termed to be an act constituting misconduct.
7. The impugned order is being assailed on the following grounds, amongst other.

- That the petitioner being a permanent employee of the respondent company, his services could not be terminated without holding an enquiry under the rules applicable to the employees of the company.
- That the principle of natural justice has been contravened by the respondents in not giving to the petitioner, any opportunity of being heard.
- That the impugned order is otherwise also erroneous and unsustainable, as it does not contain any reason and is a non-speaking order.
- That the impugned order is arbitrary and contravenes Article 14 of the Constitution.

- ....
- ....

8. That the petitioner has not filed any petition in other proceedings relating to the matter as this petition in any other court.

Prayer

In the fact and circumstances stated above, the petitioner prays that a direction in the form of a writ of *quo warranto* and *mandamus* or any other appropriate writ be issued quashing the impugned order and reinstating the petitioner in service with all consequential benefits including back wages.

It is further prayed that the respondent be burdened with costs.

Petitioner
through
Counsel

Mr. ....

Dated...................
Reference: www.icsi.edu

Annexure 6

Model Forms

Suit for Damages for Infringement of Copyright

Form No. 1

The plaintiff above named begs to state as under:

1. That the plaintiff is a novelist and a short-story writer of great repute enjoying immense popularity amongst the reading public of Hindi literature.
2. That the plaintiff is the author of about 25 novels and 150 short-stories which have a very large sale in the country.
3. That the plaintiff has written a new novel under the name and title of……………………..
4. That the defendant is the owner of a printing press called……………And has also published a number of books.
5. That the defendant on ……………………approached the plaintiff for the publication of the aforesaid new novel of the plaintiff and wanted the manuscript for his perusal so that he may then tell his terms and conditions.
6. That after about two months the defendant returned the manuscript to the plaintiff saying that it would not be possible for him to print and publish the new novel of the plaintiff as he thought that the new novel would not enjoy good sale.
7. That on…………the plaintiff found that the defendant has put on for sale a novel under the name and title of……………………which is an exact reproduction of the aforesaid new novel of the plaintiff, with changes in the names of the character, in the name of the locations and some other minor and insignificant changes. Both the books are filed herewith for comparison.

8. That the defendant has, in the circumstances narrated above, infringed the copyrights of the plaintiff in his new novel and is liable to pay damages of ₹........to the plaintiff for the same.
9. That the plaintiff is also entitled to a permanent injunction against the defendant restraining him from printing publishing and selling, of his novel above named and also to forfeiture of the books already printed and published by the defendant.
10. That the cause of action for the suit arose on.......... when the plaintiff came to know of the infringement of his copyright at..................Within the jurisdiction of this court and this court has got the jurisdiction to try the suit.
11. Valuation.
12. Relief to be claimed.

Verification:
Affidavit:

Form No. 2

Written statement to the plaint: Form No. 1

Written statement of the defendant above-named is as under:

1. The contents of Para No. 1 of the plaint are not admitted.
2. The contents of Para No. 2 of the plaint are not admitted for want of knowledge.
3. The contents of Para No. 3 of the plaint are not admitted for want of knowledge.
4. The contents of Para No. 4 of the plaint are not admitted.
5. The contents of Para No. 5 of the plaint are not denied.
6. The contents of Para No. 6 of the plaint are denied.
7. In Para No. 7 of the plaint, it is admitted that the defendant has put on for sale a novel in the name and title of...................... and the rest is denied.
8. The contents of Para No. 8 of the plaint are denied.
9. The contents of Para No. 9 of the plaint are denied.

10. The contents of Para Nos.10 and 11 of the plaint need no reply.
11. The plaintiff is not entitled to the reliefs claimed.

- Additional pleas

12. That the book..............which the defendant has published and put on for the sale is an original work of Sri......................who is a novelist of great repute and popularity, and it appears that the plaintiff has based his novel on the story of the novel published by the defendant after making some minor changes of name and place etc.
13. The plaintiff's suit is liable to be dismissed with cost to the defendant.

Verification and affidavit:

Suit for Damages for Malicious Prosecution
Form No. 3

The plaintiff above named begs to state as under:

1. That the plaintiff is a respectable man and a medical practitioner of repute of this town.
2. That the defendant lodged a report with the police station kotwali against the plaintiff under Section 420, I.P.C...........(dated) and followed it up by filing a complaint under Section 420, I.P.C., against the plaintiff in the Court of the Chief Judicial Magistrate (city).........who on........summoned the plaintiff to stand trial.
3. That after a full trial which lasted for.......hearing the Chief Judicial Magistrate (city) was pleased to acquit the plaintiff by his judgment dated........
4. That the report and the complaint of the defendant were based on absolutely false allegations and the defendant acted maliciously and without reasonable or probable cause in lodging the same.
5. That many persons, including a large number of the plaintiff's patients, hearing of the prosecution of the

plaintiff for cheating, and supposing the plaintiff to be a criminal, have ceased to be treated by and have dealings with the plaintiff, whereby the plaintiff has suffered considerable and substantial monetary loss.

6. That in consequence of the said prosecution, the plaintiff suffered physical pain and mental shock and was prevented from transacting his business and profession besides being injured in his credit and reputation.
7. That the plaintiff incurred an expenditure of ₹.......in defending himself against the defendant's said complaint.
8. That the plaintiff is entitled to recover from the defendant as damages the amounts detailed below:

- On account of loss of business and profession, ₹.....
- On account of loss of reputation and credit, ₹.......
- On account of bodily and mental pain, ₹.......
- On account of expenses of defence, ₹........
- Total ₹..........

9. That the plaintiff sent a notice to the defendant demanding payment of the aforesaid amount of ₹......The notice was served on the defendant on...... but he sent no reply.
10. That the cause of action arose on.......the date on which the plaintiff was acquitted, at..........Within the jurisdiction of this court which has jurisdiction to try this suit.
11. That the valuation of the suit for the purpose of jurisdiction and payment of court fee is ₹.......And *ad valorem* court-fee has been paid accordingly.

The plaintiff, therefore, claims the following reliefs:

1. A decree of ₹......may kindly be passed in favour of the plaintiff and against the defendant.
2. *Pendente lite* and future interest be awarded.
3. Costs of the suit may be awarded to the plaintiff against the defendant.
4. Any other relief that this Court deems just and proper may be allowed to the plaintiff.

Verification:
Affidavit:

Form No. 4

Written statement to the plaint: Form No. 3

Written statement of the defendant above named is as under:

1. The contents of Para No. 1 of the plaint are not admitted.
2. The contents of Para No. 2 of the plaint are admitted.
3. The contents of Para No. 3 of the plaint are admitted.
4. The contents of Para No. 4 of the plaint are denied.
5. The contents of Para No. 5 of the plaint are denied.
6. The contents of Para No. 6 of the plaint are denied.
7. The contents of Para No. 7 of the plaint are not admitted.
8. The contents of Para No. 8 of the plaint are denied.
9. The contents of Para No. 9 of the plaint are admitted.
10. The contents of Para Nos. 10 and 11 of the plaint need no reply.
11. The plaintiff is not entitled to reliefs claimed.

    Additional Pleas
12. That the defendant lodged the report with the police and followed it up by filing a complaint against the plaintiff under Section 420, I.P.C. in the court of the Chief Judicial Magistrate on true and correct facts.
13. That the defendant never acted maliciously and without reasonable and probable cause.
14. That the complaint filed by the defendant against the plaintiff resulted in acquittal of the plaintiff on account of the plaintiff having won over the witness of the defendant by corrupt practices of giving them bribes and treating them with drink and dinners.
15. That it will be evident from the judgment of the Chief Judicial Magistrate City..............That the plaintiff was acquitted because the Munsif Magistrate City did not consider it safe to convict the plaintiff on the sole testimony of the defendant.

16. That the plaintiff's suit is liable to be dismissed with costs to the defendant.

Verification and affidavit:

Annexure 7

Indian Easement Act, 1882

(Act No. V of 1882)

An act to define and amend the law relating to easements and licences.

Preamble: Whereas it is expedient to define and amend the law relating to easements and licences. It is hereby enacted as follows.

Preliminary

1. Short Title: This Act may be called the Indian Easements Act, 1882.

Local Extent: It extends to the territories respectively administered by the Governor of Madras in Council and the Chief Commissioners of the Central Provinces and Coorg.

Commencement: It shall come into force on the first day of July, 1882.

2. Savings: Nothing herein contained shall be deemed to affect any law not hereby expressly repealed; or to derogate from:

(a) Any right of the Government to regulate the collection, retention and distribution of the water of rivers and streams flowing in natural channels, and of natural lakes and ponds, or of the water flowing, collected, retained or distributed in or by any channel or other work constructed at the public expense for irrigation;

(b) Any customary or other right (not being a licence) in or over immovable property which the Government, the public or any person may possess irrespective of other immovable property; or

(c) Any right acquired, or arising out of a relation created, before this Act comes into force.

3. Construction of Certain References to Act XV of 1877 and Act IX of 1871: All references in any Act or Regulation to Sections 26 and 27 of the Indian Limitation Act, 1877 or to Sections 27 and 28 of Act No. IX of 1871, shall, in the territories to which this Act extends, be read as made to Sections 15 and 16 of this Act.

Chapter I: Of Easements Generally

4. Easement Defined: An easement is a right which the owner or occupier of certain land possesses, as such, for the beneficial enjoyment of that land, to do and continue to do something, or to prevent and continue to prevent something being done, in or upon, or in respect of certain other land not his own.

Dominant and Servient Heritages and Owners: The land for the beneficial enjoyment of which the right exists is called the dominant heritage, and the owner or occupier thereof the dominant owner; the land on which the liability is imposed is called the servient heritage, and the owner or occupier thereof the servient owner.

Explanation: In the first and second clauses of this section the, expression "land" includes also things permanently attached to the earth; the expression "beneficial enjoyment" includes also possible convenience, remote advantage, and even a there amenity; and the expression "to do something" includes removal and appropriation by the dominant owner, for the beneficial enjoyment of the dominant heritage, or any part of the soil of the servant heritage, or anything growing or subsisting thereon.

Illustrations:

(a) A, as the owner of a certain house, has a right of way over his neighbour B's land for purposes connected with the beneficial enjoyment of the house. This is an easement.

(b) A, as the owner of a certain house, has the right to go on his neighbour B's land and to take water for the purposes of his household, out of a spring therein. This is an easement.

(c) A, as the owner of a certain house, has the right to conduct water from B's stream to supply the fountain in the garden attached to the house. This is an easement.

(d) A, as the owner of a certain house and farm, has the right to graze a certain number of his own cattle on B's field, or to take, for the purpose of being used in the house, by himself, his family, guests, lodgers and servants, water or fish out of C's tank, or timber out of D's wood, or to use, for the purpose of manuring his land, the leaves which have fallen from the trees in E's land. These are casements.

(e) A dedicates to the public the right to occupy the surface of certain land for the purpose of passing and re-passing. This right is not an easement.

(f) A is bound to cleanse a watercourse running through his land and keep it free from obstruction for the benefit of B, a lower riparian owner. This is not easement.

5. Continuous and Discontinuous, Apparent and Non-apparent Easements: Easements are either continuous or discontinuous, apparent or non-apparent.

A continuous easement is one whose enjoyment is or may be continual without the act of man.

A discontinuous easement is one that needs the act of man for its enjoyment.

An apparent easement is one the existence of which is shown by some permanent sign, which, upon careful inspection by a competent person, would be visible to him.

A non-apparent easement is one that has no such sign.

Illustrations:

(a) A right annexed to B's house to receive light by the window without obstruction by his neighbour A. This is a continuous easement.

(b) A right of way annexed to A's house over B's land. This is a discontinuous easement.

(c) Rights annexed to A's land to lead water thither across B's land by an aqueduct and to draw off water thence by a drain. The drain would be discovered upon careful inspection by a person conversant with such matter. These are apparent easements.

(d) A right annexed to A's house to prevent B from building oil his own land. This is a non-apparent easement.

6. Easement for Limited Time or on Condition: An easement may be permanent, or for a term of years or other limited period, or subject to periodical interruption, or exercisable only at a certain place, or at certain times, or between certain hours, or for a particular purpose, or on condition that it shall commerce or become void or voidable on the happening of a specified event or the performance or non-performance of a specified Act.

7. Easement Restrictive of Certain Rights; Easements are restrictions of one or other of the following rights (namely):

(a) **Exclusive right to enjoy:** The exclusive right of every owner of immovable property (subject to any law for the time being in force) to enjoy and dispose of the same and all products thereof and accessions thereto.

(b) **Rights to advantages arising from situation:** The right of every owner of immovable property (subject to any law for the time being in force) to enjoy without disturbance by another the natural advantages arising from its situation.

Illustrations of the Rights Above Referred To:

(a) The exclusive right of every owner of land in a town to build on such land, subject to any municipal law for the time being in force.

(b) The right of every owner of land that the air passing thereto shall not be unreasonably polluted by other persons.

(c) The right of every owner of a house that his physical comfort shall not be interfered with materially and unreasonable by noise or vibration caused by any other person.

(d) The right of every owner of land to so much light and air as pass vertically thereto.

(e) The right of every owner of land that such land, in its natural conditions, shall have the support naturally rendered by the subjacent and adjacent soil of another person.

Explanation: Land is in its natural condition when it is not excavated and not subjected to artificial pressure; and the "subjacent and adjacent soil" mentioned in this illustration means such soil only as in its natural condition would support the dominant heritage in its natural condition.

(f) The right of every owner of land that, within his own limits the water which naturally passes or percolates by, over or through his land shall not before so passing or percolating, be unreasonably polluted by other persons.

(g) The right of every owner of land to collect and dispose within his own limits of all water under the land which does not pass in a defined channel and all water on its surface which does not pass in a defined channel.

(h) The right of every owner of land that the water of every natural stream which passes by through or over his land in a defined natural channel shall be allowed by other persons to flow within such owner's limits without interruption and without material attention in quantity, direction, force or temperature; the right of every owner of land abutting on a natural lake or pond into or out of which a natural stream flows, that the water of such lake or pond shall be allowed by other persons to remain within such owner's limits without material alteration in quantity or temperature.

(i) The right of every owner of upper land that water naturally rising in, or falling on such land, and not passing in defined channels, shall be allowed by the owner of adjacent lower land to run naturally thereto.

(j) The right of every owner of land abutting on a natural stream, lake or pond to use and consume its water for drinking, household purpose and watering his cattle and sheep: and the right of every such owner to use and consume the water for irrigating such land, and for the purposes of any factory situated thereon, provided that he does not thereby cause material injury to other like owners.

Explanation: A natural stream is a stream, whether permanent or intermittent, tide or tideless, on the surface of land or underground, which flows by the operation of nature only and in a natural and known course.

Chapter II: Imposition, Acquisition and Transfer of Easements

8. Who May Impose Easement?: An easement may be imposed by any one in the circumstances, and to the extent, in and to which he may transfer his interest in the heritage on which the liability is to imposed.

Illustrations:

(a) A is tenant of B's land under a lease for a period of twenty years, and has the power to transfer his interest under the lease. A may impose an easement on the land to continue during the time that the lease exists or for any shorter period.

(b) A is tenant for his life to certain land with remainder to B absolutely. A cannot unless with B's consent, impose an easement thereon which will continue after the determination of his life interest.

(c) A, B and C are co-owners of certain land. A cannot, without the consent of B and C, impose an easement on the land or on any part thereof.

(d) A and B are lessees of the same lessor, A of a field X for a term of five years and B of field Y for a term of ten years. A's interest under his lease is transferable; B's is not. A may impose on X, in favour of B, a right of way terminable with A's lease.

9. Servient Owners: Subject to the provisions of Section 8, a servient owner may impose on the servient heritage any easement that does not lessen the utility of the existing easement. But he cannot, without the consent of the dominant owner, impose an easement on the servient heritage which would lessen such utility.

Illustrations:

(a) A has, in respect of his mill, a right to the uninterrupted flow thereto, from sunrise to noon, of the water of B's stream. B may grant to C the right to divert the water of the stream from noon to sunsets, provided that A's supply is not thereby diminished.

(b) A has, in respect of his house, a right of way over B's land. B may grant to C as the owner of a neighboring farm, the right to feed his cattle on the grass growing on the way provided that A's right of way is not thereby obstructed.

10. Lessor and Mortgagor: Subject to the provisions of Section 8, a lessor may impose, on the property leased, any easement that does not derogate from the rights of the lessee as such, and a mortgagor may impose, on the property mortgaged, any easement that does not render the security insufficient. But a lessor or mortgagor cannot, without the consent of the lessee or mortgages, impose any other easement and such property, unless it be to take effect on the termination of the lease or the redemption of the mortgage.

Explanation: A security is insufficient within the meaning of this section unless the value of the mortgaged property exceeds by one-third, or, if consisting of building exceeds by one-half, the amount for the time being due on the mortgage.

11. Lessee: No lessee or other person having a derivative interest may impose on the property held by him as such an easement to take effect after the expiration of his own interest, or in derogation of the right of the right of the lessor or the superior proprietor.

12. Who May Acquire Easements?: An easement may be acquired by the owner of an immovable property for the beneficial enjoyment of which the right is created, or on his behalf, by any person in possession of the same.

One of two or more co-owners of immovable property may, as such, with or without the consent of the other or others, acquire an easement for the beneficial enjoyment of such property.

No lessee of immovable property can acquire, for the beneficial enjoyment of other immovable property of his own, an easement in or the property comprised in his lease.

13. Easements of Necessity and Quasi-easements: Where one person transfers or bequeaths immovable property to another.

(a) If an easement in other immovable property of the transferor or testator is necessary for enjoying the subject of the transfer or bequest, the transferee or legatee shall be entitled to such easement; or

(b) If such an easement is apparent and continuous and necessary for enjoying: the said subject as it was enjoyed when the transfer or bequest took effect, the transferee or lessee shall, unless a different intention is expressed or necessarily implied, be entitled to such easement; or

(c) If an easement in the subject of the transfer or bequest is necessary for enjoying other immovable property of the transferor or testator, the transferor or the legal representative of the testator shall be entitled to such easement; or

(d) If such an easement is apparent and continuous and necessary for enjoying the said property as it was enjoyed when the transfer or bequest took effect, the transferor, or the legal representative of the testator, shall, unless a different intention is expressed or necessarily implied be entitled to such easement.

Where a partition is made of the joint property of several persons,

(e) If an easement over the share of one of them is necessary for enjoying the share of another of them, the latter shall be entitled to such easement, or

(f) If such an easement is apparent and continuous and necessary for enjoying the share of the latter as it was enjoyed when the partition took effect, he shall, unless the different intention is expressed or necessary implied, be entitled to such easement.

The easements mentioned in this section, clauses (a), (c) and (e), are called easements of necessity.

Where immovable property passed by operation of law, the persons from and to whom it so passes are, for the purpose of this section, to be deemed respectively, the transferor and transferee.

Illustrations:

(a) A sells B a field to be used for agricultural purposes only. It is inaccessible except by passing over A's adjoining land or by trespassing on the land of a stranger. B is entitled to a right of way, for agricultural purposes only, over A's adjoining land to the field sold.

(b) A, the owner of two fields, sells one to B, and retains the other. The field retained was, at the date of the sale, used for agricultural purposes only, and is inaccessible except by passing over the field. A is entitled to a right of way, for agricultural purposes only, over B's field for the field retained.

(c) A sells B a house with windows overlooking A's land which A retains. The right which passes over A's land to the windows is necessary for enjoying the house as it was enjoyed when the sale took effect. B is entitled to the light, and A cannot afterwards obstruct it by building on his land.

(d) A sells B a house with windows overlooking A's land. The light passing over A's land to the windows is necessary for enjoying the house as it was enjoyed when the sale took effect. Afterwards A sells the land to C. Here C cannot obstruct the light by building on the land for it takes subject to the burdens to which it was subject in A's hands.

(e) A is the owner of a house and adjoining land. The house has windows overlooking the land. A simultaneously sells the house to B and the land to C. The light passing over the land is necessary for enjoying the house as it was enjoyed when the sale took effect. Here A impliedly grants B a right to the light, and C takes the land subject to the restriction that he may not build so as to obstruct such light.

(f) A is the owner of a house and adjoining land. The house has windows overlooking the land. A, retaining the house sells the land to B, without expressly reserving any easement. The light passing over the land is necessary for enjoying the house as it was enjoyed when the sale took effect. A is entitled to the light and B cannot build on the land so as to obstruct such light.

(g) A, the owner of a house, sells B a factory built on adjoining land. B is entitled, as against A, to pollute the air, when necessary, with smoke and vapours from the factory.

(h) A, the owner of two adjoining houses, Y and Z, sells Y to B, and retains Z. B is entitled to the benefit of all gutters and drains common to the two houses and necessary for enjoying Y as it was enjoyed when the sale took effect, and A is entitled to the benefit of all the gutters and drains common to the two houses and necessary for enjoying Z as it was enjoyed when the sale took effect.

(i) A, the owner of two adjoining buildings, sells one to B, while retaining the other. B is entitled to right to lateral support from A's building, and A is entitled to a right to lateral support from in B's building.

(j) A, the owner of two adjoining building, sells one to B, and the other to C. C is entitled to lateral support from B's building, and B is entitled to lateral support from C's building.

(k) A grants lands to B for the purpose of building a house thereon. B is entitled to such amount of lateral and subjacent support from A's land as is necessary for the safety of the house.

(l) Under the Land Acquisition Act, 1870, a railway company compulsorily acquires a portion of B's land for the purpose of making a siding. The company is entitled to such amount of lateral support from B's adjoining land as is essential for the safety of the siding.

(m) Owing to the partition of joint property, A becomes the owner of an upper room in a building, and B becomes the owner of the portion of the building immediately beneath it. A is entitled to such amount of vertical support from B's portion as is essential for the safety of the upper room.

(n) A lets a house and ground to B for a particular business. B has no access in them other than by crossing A's land. B is entitled to a right of way over that land suitable to the business to be carried on by B in the house and ground.

14. Direction of Way of Necessity: When a right to a way of necessity is created under Section 13, the transferor, the legal representative of the testator, or the owner of the share over which the right is exercised, as the case may be, is entitled to set out the way but it must be reasonably convenient for the dominant owner.

When the person so entitled to set out the way refuses or neglects to do so, the dominant owner may set it out.

15. Acquisition by Prescription: Where the access and use of light or air and for any building have been peaceably enjoyed therewith, as an easement, without interruption, and for twenty years.

And where support from one person's land or things affixed thereto, has been peaceably, received by another person's land subjected to artificial pressure, or by things affixed thereto, as an easement, without interruption, and for twenty years,

And where a right of way or any other easement has been peaceably and openly enjoyed by any person claiming title thereto, as an easement and as of right, without interruption, and for twenty years,

The right, to such access and use of light or air, support, or other easement, shall be absolute.

Each of the said periods of twenty years shall be taken to be a period ending within two years next before the institution of the suit wherein the claim to which such period relates is contested.

Explanation I: Nothing is an enjoyment within the meaning of this section when it has been had in pursuance of an agreement with the owner or occupier of the property over which the right is claimed, and it is apparent from the agreement that such right has not been granted as an easement, or, if granted as an easement, that it has been granted for a limited period, or subject to a condition on the fulfilment of which it is to cease.

Explanation II: Nothing is an interruption within the meaning of this section unless where there is an actual cessation of the enjoyment by reason of an obstruction by the act of some other than the claimant, and unless such obstruction is submitted to or acquiesced in for one year after the claimant has notice thereof, and of the person making or authorizing the same to be made.

Explanation III: Suspensions of enjoyment in pursuance of a contract between the dominant and servient owners is not an interruption within the meaning of the section.

Explanation IV: In the case of an easement to pollute water, the said period of twenty years begins when the pollution first prejudices perceptibly the servient heritage.

When the property over which a right is claimed under this section belongs to the Government, this section shall be read as if for the words "twenty years" the words "thirty years" were substituted.

Illustrations:

(a) A suit is brought in 1883 for obstructing a right of way. The defendant admits the abduction but denies the right of way. The plaintiff proves that the right was peaceably and openly enjoyed by him, claiming title thereto, as an easement, and as of right, without interruption, from 1st January, 1862, to 1st January, 1882. The plaintiff is entitled to judgment.

(b) In a like suit the plaintiff shows that the right was peaceably and openly enjoyed by him for twenty years. The defendant proves that for a year of that time the plaintiff was entitled to possession of the servient heritage as lessee thereof and enjoyed the right as such lessee. The suit shall be dismissed, for the right of way has not been enjoyed "as an easement" for twenty years.

(c) In a like suit the plaintiff shows that the right was peaceably and openly enjoyed by him for twenty years. The defendant proves that the plaintiff on one occasion during the twenty years had admitted that the user was not of right and asked his leave to enjoy the right. The suit shall be dismissed, for the right of way has not been enjoyed "as of right" for twenty years.

16. Exclusion in Favour of Reversioner of Servient Heritage: Provided that, when any land upon, over or from which any easement has been enjoyed or derived, has been held under or by virtue of any interest for life or any term of years exceeding three years from the granting thereof, the time of the enjoyment of such easement during the continuance of such interest or term shall be excluded in the computation of the said last-mentioned period of twenty years in case the claim is, within three years next after the determination of such, interest or term, resisted by the person entitled, on such determination, to the said land.

Illustration:

(a) A sues for a declaration that he is entitled to a right of way over B's land. A proves that he has enjoyed the right for twenty-five years. But B shows that during ten of these years, C had a life-interest in the land; that on death B became entitled to the land; and that within two years after C's death lie contested A's claim to the right. The suit must be dismissed, as A, with reference to the provisions of this section, has only proved enjoyment for fifteen years.

17. Rights Which Cannot be Acquired by Prescription: Easements acquired under Section 15 are said to be acquired by prescription, and are called prescriptive rights.

None of the following rights can be so acquired

(a) A right which would tend to the total destruction of the subject of the right, or the property on which, if the acquisition were made, liability would be imposed.

(b) A right to the free passage of light or air to an open space of ground.

(c) A right to surface water not flowing in a stream and not permanently collected in a pool, tank or otherwise.

(d) A right to underground water not passing in a defined channel.

18. Customary Easements: An easement may be acquired in virtue of a local custom. Such easements are called customary easements.

Illustrations:

(a) By the custom of a certain village, every cultivator of village land is entitled, as such, to graze his cattle on the common pasture. A having become the tenant of a plot of uncultivated land in the village breaks up and cultivates that plot he thereby acquires an easement to graze his cattle in accordance with the custom.

(b) By the custom of a certain town, no owner or occupier of a house can open a new window therein so as substantially to invade his neighbor's privacy. A builds a house in the town near B's house. A thereupon acquires an easement that B shall not open new windows in his house so as to command a view of the portions of A's house which are ordinarily excluded from observation, and B requires a like easement with respect to A's house.

19. Transfer of Dominant Heritage Passes Easement: Where the dominant heritage is transferred or devolves, by act of parties or by operation of law, the transfer or revolution shall, unless a contrary intention appears, be deemed to pass the easement to the person in whose favour the transfer or devolution takes place.

Illustration:

A has certain land to which a right of way is annexed. A lets the land to B for twenty years. The right of way vests in B and his legal representatives so long as the lease continues.

Chapter III: Incidents of Easements

20. Rules Controlled by Contract or Title: The rules contained in this Chapter are controlled by any contract between the dominant and servient owners relating to the servient heritage, and by the provisions of the instrument or decree, if any, by which the easement referred to was imposed.

Incidents of Customary Easements: And when any incident of any customary easement is inconsistent with such rules, nothing in this Chapter shall affect such incident.

21. Bar to Use Unconnected with Enjoyment: An easement must not be used for any purpose not connected with the enjoyment of the dominant heritage.

Illustrations:

(a) A, as owner of a farm Y, has right of way over B's land to Y. Lying beyond Y, A has another farm Z the beneficial enjoyment of which is not necessary for the beneficial enjoyment of Y. He must not use the easement for the purpose of passing to and from Z.

(b) A, as owner of a certain house, has a right of way to and from it. For the purpose of passing to and from the house, the right may be used, not only by A, but by the members of his family, his guests, lodgers, servants, workmen, visitors and customers: for this is a purpose, connected with the enjoyment of the dominant heritage. So, if A lets the house, he may use the right of way for the purpose of collecting the rent and seeing that the house is kept in repair.

22. Exercise of Easement: Confinement of Exercise of Easement: The dominant owner must exercise his right in the mode which is least onerous to the servient owner; and, when the exercise of an easement can without any detriment to the dominant owner be, confined to a determinate part of the servient heritage, such exercise shall, at the request of the servient owner be so confined.

Illustrations:

(a) A has a right of way over B's field, A must enter the way at either end and not at any intermediate point.

(b) A has a right annexed to his house to cut thatching grass in B's swamp. A when exercising his easement must cut the grass so that the plants may not be destroyed.

23. Right to Alter Made of Enjoyment: Subject to the provisions of Section 22, the dominant owner may, from time to time, alter the mode and place of enjoying the easement provided that he does not thereby impose any additional burden on the servient heritage.

Exception: The dominant owner of a right of way cannot vary his line of passage at pleasure, even though he does not thereby impose any additional burden on the servient heritage.

Illustrations:

(a) A, the owner of a sawmill, has a right to a flow of water sufficient to run the mill. He may convert the saw mill into a corn-mill; provided that it can be worked by the same amount of water.

(b) A has a right to discharge in B's land the rain water from the eaves of A's house. This does not entitle A to advance his eaves if, by so doing, he imposes a greater burden on B's land.

(c) A as the owner of a paper mill, acquires a right to pollute a stream in the refuse-liquor produced by making in the mill paper from rags. He may pollute the stream by pouring similar liquor produced by making in the mill paper by a new process from bamboos, provided that he does not substantially increase the amount, or injuriously change of the pollution.

(d) A, a riparian owner, acquires as against the lower riparian owners, a prescriptive right to pollute a stream by throwing saw dust into it. This does not entitle A to pollute by discharging into it poisonous liquor.

24. Right to Do Acts to Secure Enjoyment: The dominant owner is entitled, against the servient owner, to do all acts necessary to secure the full enjoyment of the easement; but such acts must be done at such time and in such a manner as, without detrimental to the dominant owner, to cause the servient owner as little inconvenience as possible; and the dominant owner must repair, as far practicable, the damage (if any) caused by the act to the servient heritage.

Accessory Rights: Rights to do acts necessary to secure the full enjoy easement are called accessory rights.

Illustrations:

(a) A has air easement to lay pipes in B's land to convey water to A's cistern. A may enter a dig tire land in order to mend tire pipes, but he must restore the surface to its original state.

(b) A has an easement of a drain through B's land. The sewer with which the drain communicates is altered. A may enter upon B's land and alter the drain, to adapt it to the new sewer, provided that he does not thereby impose any additional burden on B's land.

(c) A, as owner of a certain house, has a right of way over B's land. The way is out of repair or a tree is blown down and falls across it. A may enter on B's land and repair the way or remove the tree from it.

(d) A, as owner of a certain field, has a right of way over B's land. B renders the way impassable. A may deviate from the way and pass over the adjoining land of B provided that the deviation is reasonable.

(e) A, as owner of a certain house, has a right of way over B's field. A may remove rocks to make the way.

(f) A has an easement of support from B's wall. The wall gives way. A may enter upon B's land and repair the wall.

(g) A has an easement to have his land flooded by means of a dam in B's stream. The dam is half swept by an inundation. A may enter upon B's land and repair the dam.

25. Liability for Expenses Necessary for Preservation of Easement: The expenses incurred in constructing works, or making repairs, or doing any other act necessary for the use or preservation of an easement, must be defrayed by the dominant owner.

26. Liability for Damage for Want of Repair: Where an easement is enjoyed by means of an artificial work, the dominant owner is liable to make compensation of any damage to the servient heritage arising from the want of repair of such work.

27. Servient Owner not Bound to do Anything: The servient owner is not bound to do anything for the benefit of the dominant heritage, and he is entitled, as against the dominant owner, to use the servient heritage in any way consistent with the enjoyment of the easement; but he must not do any act tending to restrict the easement or to render its exercise less convenient.

Illustrations:

(a) A, as owner of a house, has a fight to lead water and send sewage through B's land. B is not bound, as servient owner, to clear the watercourse or scour tire sewer.

(b) A grants a right of way through his land to B as owner of a field. A may feed his cattle on grass growing on the way, provided that B's right of way is not thereby obstructed; but A must not build a wall at the end of his land so as to prevent B from going beyond it, nor must he narrow the way so as to render the exercise of the right less easy than it was at the date of the grant.

(c) A, in respect of his house, is entitled to an easement of support from B's wall. B is not bound, as servient owner to keep the wall standing and in repair. But he must not pull down or weaken the wall so as to make it incapable of rendering the necessary support.

(d) A, in respect of his mill, is entitled to a watercourse through B's land. A must not drive stakes so as to obstruct the watercourse.

(e) A, in respect of his house, is entitled to a certain quantity of light passing over B's land. B must not plant trees so as to obstruct the passage to A's windows of that quantity of light.

28. Extent of Easements: With respect to the extent of easements and the mode of their enjoyment, the following provisions shall take effect:

Easement of Necessity: An easement of necessity is co-extensive with the necessity, as it existed when the easement was imposed.

Other Easements: The extent of any other easement and the mode of its enjoyment must be fixed with reference to the probable intention of the parties, and the purpose for which the right was imposed or acquired.

In the absence of evidence as to such intention and purpose:

(a) **Right of Way: A** right of way of any one kind does not include a right of way of any other kind.

(b) **Right of Light or Air Acquired by Grant:** The extent of a right to the passage of light or air to a certain window, door on other opening, imposed by a testamentary or non-testamentary instrument, is the quantity of light or air that entered the opening at the time the testator died or the non-testamentary instrument was made.

(c) **Prescriptive Right to Light or Air:** The extent of a prescriptive right to the passage of light or air to a certain window, door or other opening is that quantity of light or air which has been accustomed to enter that opening during the whole of the perceptive period irrespective of the purposes for which it has been used.

(d) **Prescriptive Right to Pollute Air or Water:** The extent of a prescriptive right to pollute air or water is the extent of the pollution at the commencement of the period of user on completion of which the right arose.

(e) **Other Prescriptive Rights:** The extent of every other prescriptive right to pollute air or water is the extent of the pollution at the commencement of the period of user or completion of which the right arose.

(f) **Other Prescriptive Rights:** The extent of every other prescriptive right and the mode of its enjoyment must be determined by the accustomed user of the right.

29. Increase of Easement: The dominant owner cannot, by merely altering or adding to the dominant heritage, substantially increase an easement.

Where an easement has been granted or bequeathed so that its extent shall be proportionate to the extent of the dominant heritage, if the dominant heritage is increased by alluvion, the easement is proportionately increased, and if the dominant heritage is diminished by diluvion, the easement is proportionately diminished.

Save as aforesaid, no easement is effected by any change in the extent of the dominant or the servient heritage.

Illustrations:

(a) A, the owner of a mill, has acquired a prescriptive right, to divert to his mill, part of the water of a stream. A alters the machinery of his mill. He cannot thereby increase his right to divert water.

(b) A has acquired an easement to pollute a stream by carrying on a manufacture on its banks by which a certain quantity of foul matter is discharged into it. A extends his works and thereby increases the quantity discharged. He is responsible to the lower riparian owners for injury done by such an increase.

(c) A as the owner of a farm, has a right to take for the purpose of manuring his farm, leaves which have fallen from the trees on B's land. A buys a field and unites it to his farm. A is not thereby entitled to take leaves to manure his fields.

30. Partition of Dominant Heritage: Where a dominant heritage is divided between two or more persons, the easement becomes annexed to each of the shares, but not so as to increase substantially the burden on the servient heritage: provided that such annexation is consistent with the terms of the instrument, decree or revenue proceeding (if any) under which the division was made, and in the case of prescriptive rights, with the user during the prescriptive period.

Illustrations:

(a) A house to which a right of way by a particular path is annexed is divided into two parts, one of which is granted to A, the other to B. Each is entitled, in respect of his part, to a right of way by the same path.

(b) A house to which is annexed the right of drawing water from a well to the extent of fifty buckets a day is divided into two distinct heritages, one of which is granted to A, the other to B. A and B are each entitled, in respect of this heritage, to draw from the well fifty buckets a day but the amount drawn by both must not exceed fifty buckets a day.

(c) A, having in respect of his house an easement of light, divides the house into three district heritages. Each of these continues to have the right to have its windows unobstructed.

31. Obstruction in Case of Excessive User: In the case of excessive user of an easement the servient owner may, without prejudice to any other remedies to which he may be entitled, obstruct the user but only on the servient heritage. Provided that such user cannot be obstructed when the obstruction would interfere with the lawful enjoyment of the easement.

Illustrations:

A, having a right to the free passage over B's land of light to four windows, 6'x 4', increases their size and number. It is impossible to obstruct the passage of light to the new windows without also obstructing the passage of light to the ancient windows. B cannot obstruct the excessive user.

Chapter IV: Disturbance of Easements

32. Right to Enjoyment without Disturbance: The owner or occupier of the dominant heritage is entitled to enjoy the easement without disturbance by any other person.

Illustration:

A, as owner of a house, has a right of way over B's land. C unlawfully enters on B's land and obstructs A in his right of way. A may use C for compensation, not for the entry, but for the obstruction.

33. Suit for Disturbance of Easement: The owner of any interest in the dominant heritage, or the occupier of such heritage, may institute a suit for compensation for the disturbance of the easement or of any right accessory thereto: provided that the disturbance has actually caused substantial damage to the plaintiff.

Explanation I: The doing of any act likely to injure the plaintiff by affecting the evidence of the easement, or by materially diminishing the value of the dominant heritage, is substantial damage within the meaning of this section and Section 34.

Explanation II: Where the easement disturbed is a right to the free passage of light passing to the openings in a house, no damage is substantial within the meaning of this section unless it falls within the first explanation, or interferes materially with the physical comfort of the plaintiff, or prevents him from carrying on his accustomed business in the dominant heritage as beneficially as he had done previously to instituting the suit.

Explanation III: Where the easement disturbed is a right to the free passage of light to the openings in a house, damage is substantial within the meaning of this section if it interferes materially with the physical comfort of the plaintiff, though it is not injurious to his health.

Illustrations:

(a) A places a permanent obstruction in a path over which B, as tenant of C's house, has a right of way. This is a substantial damage to C, for it may affect the evidence of his reversionary right to the easement.

(b) A, as owner of a house, has a right to walk along one side of B's house. B builds a verandah overhanging the way about ten feet from the ground and so as not to occasion any inconvenience to foot passengers using the way. This is not a substantial damage to A.

34. When Cause of Action Arises for Removal of Support: The removal of the means of support to which a dominant owner is entitled does not give rise to a right to recover compensation unless and until substantial damage is actually sustained.

35. Injunction to Restrain Disturbance: Subject to the provisions the Specific Relief Act, 1877, Sections 52 to 57 (both inclusive), an injunction may be granted to restrain the disturbance of an easement.

(a) If the easement is actually disturbed, then compensation for such disturbance might be recovered under this Chapter.

(b) If the disturbance is only threatened or intended, then the act threatened or intended must necessarily, if performed, disturbs the easement.

36. Abatement of Obstruction of Easement: Notwithstanding the provisions of Section 24, the dominant owner cannot himself abate a wrongful obstruction of an easement.

Chapter V: Extinction, Suspension and Revival of Easement

37. Extinction by Dissolution of Right of Servient Owner: When, from a cause which preceded the imposition of an easement, the person by whom it was imposed, ceases to have any right in the servient heritage, the easement is extinguished.

Exception: Nothing in this section applies to an easement lawfully imposed by a mortgagor in accordance with Section 10.

Illustrations:

(a) A transfers Sultanpur to B on condition that he does not marry C, B impresses an easement on Sultanpur. Then B marries C, B's interest in Sultanpur ends, and with it the easement is extinguished.

(b) A, in 1860, let Sultanpur to B for thirty years from the date of the lease. B, in 1861, imposes an easement on the land in favour of C, who enjoys the easement peaceably and openly an easement without interruption for twenty nine years, B's interest in Sultanpur then ends, and with it C's easement.

(c) A and B, tenants of C, have permanent transferable interest in their respective holdings. A imposes on his holding an easement to draw water from a tank for the purpose of irrigating B's land. B enjoys the easement for twenty years. Then A's rent falls into arrear and his interest is sold, B's easement is extinguished.

(d) A mortgages Sultanpur to B and lawfully imposes an easement on the land in favour of C in accordance with the provisions of Section 10. The land is sold to D in satisfaction of the mortgage debt. The easement is not thereby extinguished.

38. Extinction by Release: An easement is extinguished when the dominant owner releases it, expressly or impliedly, to the servient owner.

Such release can be made only in the circumstances and to the extent in and to which the dominant owner can alienate the dominant heritage.

An easement may be released as to part only of the servient heritage.

Explanation I: An easement is impliedly released:

(a) Where the dominant owner expressly authorises an act of a permanent nature to be done on the servient heritage, the necessary consequence of which is to prevent his future enjoyment of the easement, and such act is done in pursuance of such authority.

(b) Where any permanent alteration is made in the dominant heritage of such a nature as to show that the dominant owner intended to cease to enjoy the easement in future.

Explanation II: Mere non-use of an easement is not an implied release within the meaning of this section.

Illustrations:

(a) A, B and C are co-owners of a house to which an easement is annexed. A, without the consent of B and C releases the easement. This release is effectual only all against A and his legal representative.

(b) A grants B an easement over A's land for the beneficial enjoyment of his house. B assigned the house to C, B then purports to release the easement. The release is ineffectual.

(c) A, having the right to discharge his eavesdropping into B's yard, expressly authorises B to build over this year to a height which will interfere with the discharge. B builds accordingly; A's easement is extinguished to the extent of the interference.

(d) A, having an easement of light to a window, builds up that window with bricks and mortar so as to manifest an intention to abandon the easement permanently. The easement is impliedly in release.

(e) A, having a projecting roof by means of which he enjoys an easement to discharge eavesdropping on B's land permanently alters the roof so as to direct the rain-water into a different channel and discharge it on C's land. The easement is impliedly released.

39. Extinction by Revocation: An easement is extinguished when the servient owner, in exercise of power reserved in this behalf, revokes the easement.

40. Extinction on Expiration of Limited Period or Happening of Dissolving Condition: An easement is extinguished where it has been imposed for a limited period, or acquired on condition that it shall become void on the performance or non-performance of a specified act and the period expires or the condition is fulfilled.

41. Extinction on Termination of Necessity: An easement of necessity is extinguished when the necessity comes to an end.

Illustrations:

(a) A grants B a field inaccessible except by passing over A's adjoining land, B afterwards purchases a part of that land over which he can pass to his field. The right of way over A's land which B has acquired is extinguished.

42. Extinction of Useless Easement: An easement is extinguished when it becomes incapable of being at any time and under any circumstances beneficial to the dominant owner.

43. Extinction by Permanent Change in Dominant Heritage: Whereby, any permanent change in the dominant heritage, the burden on the servient heritage is materially increased and cannot be reduced by the servient owner without interfering with the lawful enjoyment of the easement, the easement is extinguished unless:

(a) It was intended for the beneficial enjoyment of the dominant heritage, to whatever extent the easement should be used; or

(b) The injury caused to the servient owner by the change is so slight that no reasonable person would complain of it; or

(c) The easement is an easement of necessity.

Nothing in this section shall be deemed to apply to in easement entitling the dominant owner in support of the dominant heritage.

44. Extinction on Permanent Alteration of Servient Heritage by Superior Force: An easement is extinguished where the servient heritage is by superior force so permanently altered that dominant owner can no longer enjoy such easement.

Provided that, where a way of necessity is destroyed by superior force, the dominant owner has a right to another way over the servient heritage; and the provisions of Section 14 apply to such way.

Illustrations:

(a) A grants to B, as the owner of a certain house, a right to fish in a river running through A's land. The river changes its course permanently and runs through C's land. B's easement is extinguished.

(b) Access to a path over which A has a right of way is permanently cut off by an earthquake. A's right is extinguished.

45. Extinction by Destruction of Either Heritage: An easement is extinguished when either the dominant or the servient heritage is completely destroyed.

Illustration:

A has a right of way over a road running along the foot of a sea-cliff. The road is washed away by a permanent encroachment of the sea. A's easement is extinguished.

46. Extinction by Unity of Ownership: An easement is extinguished when the same person becomes entitled to the absolute ownership of the whole of the dominant and servient heritages.

Illustrations:

(a) A, as the owner of a house, has a right of way over B's field. A mortgages his house, and B mortgages his field to C. Then C forecloses both mortgages and becomes thereby the absolute owner of both house and field. The right of way is extinguished.

(b) The dominant owner acquires only part of the servient heritage: the easement is not extinguished, except in the ease illustrated in Section 41.

(c) The servient owner acquires the dominant heritage in connection with a person; the easement is not extinguished.

(d) The separate owners of two separate dominant heritages jointly acquire the heritage which is servient to the two separate heritages; the easements are not extinguished.

(e) The joint owners of the dominant heritage jointly acquire the servient heritage; the easement is extinguished.

(f) A single right of way exists over two servient heritages for the beneficial enjoyment of a single dominant heritage. The dominant owner acquires only one of the servient heritages. The easement is not extinguished.

(g) A has a right of way over B's road. B dedicates the road to the public. A's right of way is not extinguished.

47. Extinction by Non-enjoyment: A continuous easement is extinguished when it totally ceases to be enjoyed as such for an unbroken period of twenty years.

A discontinuous easement is extinguished when, for a like period, it has not been enjoyed as such.

Such period shall be reckoned, in the case of a continuous easement, from the day on which its enjoyment, was obstructed by the servient owner or rendered impossible by the dominant owner; and, in the case of a discontinuous easement, from the day on which it was last enjoyed by the person as dominant owner:

Provided that if, in the case of a discontinuous easement the dominant owner, within such period, registers, under the Indian Registration Act, III of 1877, a declaration of his intention to retain such easement, it shall not be extinguished until a period of twenty years has elapsed from the date of the registration.

Where an easement can be legally enjoyed only at a certain place, or at certain times, or between certain hours, or for a particular purpose, enjoyment during the said period at another place, or at other items, or between other hours, or for another purpose, does not prevent is extinction under this section.

The circumstance that, during the said period no one was in possession of the servient heritage, or that the easement could not be enjoyed or that a right accessory thereto was enjoyed, or that dominant owner was not aware of its existence, or that he enjoyed it in ignorance of his right to do so, does not prevent its extinction under this section.

An easement is not extinguished under this section:

(a) Where the cessation is in pursuance of contract between the dominant and servient owners.

(b) Where the dominant heritage is held in co-ownership, and one of the co-owners enjoys the easement within the said period; or

(c) Where the easement is necessary easement.

Where several heritages are respectively subject to rights of way for the benefit of a single heritage, and the ways are continuous, such rights shall, for the purposes of this section, be deemed to be a single easement.

Illustration: A has, an X to his house, rights of way from the high road neither over the heritages X and Z and the intervening heritage Y. Before the twenty years expire, A exercises his right of way over X. His rights of way over Y and Z are not extinguished.

48. Extinction of Accessory Right: When an easement is extinguished, the right (if any) of accessory thereto are also extinguished.

Illustration:

A has an easement to draw water from B's well. As accessory thereto A has a right of way over B's land to and from the well. The easement to draw water is extinguished under Section 47. The right of way is also extinguished.

49. Suspension of easement: An easement is suspended when the dominant owner becomes entitled to possession of the servient heritage for a limited interest therein or when the servient owner becomes entitled to possession of the dominant heritage for a limited interest therein.

50. Servient Owner not Entitled to Require Continuance: The servient owner does not have the right to require that an easement be continued; and notwithstanding the provisions of Section 26, he is not entitled to compensation for damage caused to the servient heritage in consequence of the extinguishment or suspension of the easement, if the dominant owner has given to the servient owner, such notice as will enable him, without unreasonable expense, to protect the servient heritage from such damage.

Compensation for Damage Caused by Extinguishment or Suspension: When such notice has not been given, the servient owner is entitled to compensation for damage caused to the servient heritage in consequence of such extinguishment or suspension.

Illustration:

A, in exercise of an easement, diverts to his canal the water of B's stream. The diversion continues for many years, and during that time the bed of the stream partly fills up. A then abandons his easement, and restores the stream to its ancient court. B's land is consequently flooded. B sues A for compensation for the damage caused by the flooding. It is proved that A gave B a months' notice of his intention to abandon the easement, and that such notice was not sufficient to enable B, without unreasonable expense, to have prevented the damage. The suit must he dismissed.

51. Revival of Easement: An easement extinguished under Section 45 revives: (a) when the destroyed heritage is, before twenty years have expired, restored by the deposit of alluvion; (b) when the destroyed heritage is a servient building and before twenty years have expired, such building is rebuilt upon the same site, and (c) when the destroyed heritage is a dominant building and before twenty years have expired, such building is rebuilt upon the same site and in such a manner as not to impose a greater burden on the servient heritage.

An easement extinguished under Section 46, revives when the grant or bequest by which the unity of ownership was produced is set aside by the decree of a competent court. A necessary easement extinguished under the same section revives when the unity of ownership ceases from any other cause.

A suspended easement revives if the cause of suspension is removed before the right is extinguished under Section 47.

Illustration:

A, as the absolute owner of field Y, has right of way over B's field. A obtains from B a lease of Z for twenty years. The easement is suspended so long as A remains lessee of Z. But when A assigns the lease to C, or surrenders it to B, the right of way revives.

Chapter VI: Licences

52. Licence Defined: Where one person grants to another, or to a definite number of other persons, a right to do, or continue to do, in or upon the immovable property of the grantor, something which would, in the absence of such right, be unlawful, and such right does not amount to an easement or an interest in the property, the right is called a licence.

53. Who May Grant Licence: A licence may be granted by anyone in the circumstances and to the extent in and to which he may transfer his interests in the property affected by the licence.

54. Grant May be Express or Implied: The grant of a licence may be express or implied from the conduct of the grantor, and an agreement which purports to create an easement, but is ineffectual for that purpose, may operate to create a licence.

55. Accessory Licences Annexed by Law: All licences necessary for the enjoyment of any interest, or the exercise of any right, are implied in the constitution of such interest or right. Such licences are called accessory licences.

Illustration:

A sells the trees growing in his land to B. B is entitled to go on the land and take away the trees.

56. Licence when Transferable: Unless a different intention is expressed or necessarily implied, a licence to attend a place of public entertainment may be transferred by the licensee; but, save as aforesaid, a licence cannot be transferred by the licensee or exercised by his servants or agents.

Illustrations:

(a) A grants B a right to walk over A's field whenever he pleases. The right is not annexed to any immovable property of B. The right cannot be transferred.

(b) The Government grants B a licence to erect and use temporary grain-sheds on Government land. In the absence of express provision to the contrary, B's servants may enter on the land for the purpose of erecting sheds, erect the same, deposit grain therein and remove grain therefrom.

57. Grantor's Duty to Disclose Defects: The grantor of a licence is bound to disclose to the licensee, any defect in the property affected by the licence, likely to be dangerous to the person or property of the licence of which the grantor is, and the licensee is not, aware of.

59. Grantor's Transfer not Bound by Licence: When the grantor of the licence transfers the property affected thereby, the transferee is not as such bound by the licence.

60. Licence when Revocable: A licence may be revoked by grantor, unless:

(a) It is coupled with a transfer of property and such transfer is in force.

(b) The licensee, acting upon the licence, has executed a work of a permanent character and incurred expenses in the execution.

61. Revocation Express or Implied: The revocation of a licence may be express or implied.

Illustrations:

(a) A, the owner of a field, grants a licence to B, to use a path across it. A, with the intent to revoke the licence, locks a gate across the path. The licence is revoked.

(b) A, the owner of a field, grants a licence to B to stack hay on the field. A lets or sells the field to C. The licence is revoked.

62. Licence when Deemed Revoked: A licence is deemed to be revoked:

(a) When, from a cause preceding the grant of it, the grantor ceases to have any interest in the property affected by the licence.

(b) When the licensee releases it, expressly or impliedly, to the grantor of his representative.

(c) Where it has been granted for a limited period, or acquired on condition that it shall become void on the performance or non-performance of a specified act, and the period expires, or the condition is fulfilled.

(d) Where the property affected by the licence is destroyed or by superior force so permanently altered that the licensee can no longer exercise his right.

(e) Where the licensee becomes entitled to the absolute ownership of the property affected by the licence.

(f) Where the licence is granted for a specified purpose and the purpose is attained or abandoned, or becomes impracticable.

(g) Where the licence is granted to the licensee holding a particular office, employment or character, and such office, employment or character ceases to exist.

(h) Where the licence totally ceases to be used as such for an unbroken period of twenty years and such cessation is not in pursuance of a contract between the grantor and the licensee.

(i) In the case of all accessory licence, when the interest or right to which it is accessory ceases to exist.

63. Licensee's Rights on Revocation: Where a licence is revoked, the licensee is entitled to reasonable time to leave the property affected thereby and to remove any goods which lie has been allowed to place on such property.

64. Licensee's Rights on Eviction: Where a licence has been granted for a consideration, and the licensee, without any fault of his own, is evicted by the grantor before he has fully enjoyed, under the licence, the right for which he contracted, he is entitled to recover compensation from the grantors.

Annexure 8

Motor Vehicles (MV) Act, 1988

Introduction

A motor vehicle or road vehicle is a self-propelled wheeled vehicle that does not operate on rails, such as trains or trolleys. The vehicle propulsion is provided by an engine or motor, usually by an internal combustion engine, or an electric motor, or some combination of the two, such as hybrid electric vehicles and plug-in hybrids. The word motor broadly covers various types of vehicles plying on the roads viz. two wheelers (scooters and bikes), three wheelers or four wheelers like private cars, jeeps, cabs, buses, trucks, tractors, road rollers and other miscellaneous vehicles. As of 2014, there were more than one billion vehicles in use in the world excluding off-road vehicles and heavy construction equipment. Motor vehicle insurance or motor insurance is insurance purchased for cars, trucks, motorcycles, and other road vehicles. Its primary use is to provide financial protection against physical damage and/or bodily injury resulting from traffic collisions and liability that could arise out of use of motor vehicle.

Motor insurance accounts for a major portion of miscellaneous branch of insurance of non-life insurance companies. Motor insurance being a contract like any other contract has to fulfil the requirements of a valid contract as laid down in the Indian Contract Act, 1872. In addition, it has certain special features common to other insurance contracts. They are: utmost good faith, insurable interest, indemnity, subrogation and contribution, and proximate cause. This falls under tariff class of business and premium rates are governed by All India Motor Tariff prepared by Tariff Advisory Committee. The motor tariff divides all kinds of motor vehicles into three categories:

1. Private cars.
2. Motorcycles and scooters.
3. Commercial vehicles which are further categorized as:

- Goods carrying vehicles (lorries, trucks etc.).
- Passenger carrying vehicles (buses, cabs or taxis, motorized rickshaws etc.).
- Miscellaneous vehicles (ambulances, road rollers, tippers, cinema film recording and publicity vans, mobile dispensaries etc.).

Prior to the introduction of Motor Vehicle Act, 1939, many of the pedestrians getting injured or killed because of accidents involving motor vehicles did not get any compensation as the owners of the vehicle did not have resources to pay and there used to be no insurance. This led to the introduction of compulsory insurance of all motor vehicles plying on road (except those specifically exempted) so as to safeguard the interests of all road users including pedestrians.

In India, a motor insurance, with third party liability, is compulsory under the Motor Vehicle Act, 1939, amended in 1988 and further amended in 1994.

As per Section 146 of Motor Vehicle Act, 1988 (Necessity for insurance against third party risk), "No person shall use, except as a passenger, or cause or allow any other person to use, a motor vehicle in a public place, unless there is in force in relation to the use of the vehicle by that person or that other person, as the case may be, a policy of insurance complying with the requirements of this Chapter".

Main Provisions of the Motor Vehicle Act, 1988

Some important provisions of MV Act, 1988 are explained below. For the sake of brevity, only relevant portion of some important sections, which are of use for everybody in day to day life, are given. For complete details of any section or provision, the Motor Vehicle Act, 1988 (as amended up to date) may be referred.

Section 2 (28)–Motor Vehicle or Vehicle: Motor vehicle or vehicle means any mechanically propelled vehicle adapted for use upon roads whether the power of propulsion is transmitted thereto from an external or internal source and includes a chassis to which a body has not been attached and a trailer; but does not include a vehicle running upon fixed rails or a vehicle of a special type adapted for use only in a factory or in any other enclosed premises or a vehicle having less than four wheels fitted with engine capacity of not exceeding thirty five cubic centimetres.

Section 4–Age Limit in Connection with Driving of Motor Vehicles:

1. No person under the age of eighteen years shall drive a motor vehicle in any public place provided that a motor cycle without gear may be driven in a public place by a person after attaining the age of sixteen years.
2. Subject to the provisions of Section 18, no person under the age of twenty years shall drive a transport vehicle in any public place.
3. No learner's licence or driving licence shall be issued to any person to drive a vehicle of the class to which he has made an application unless he is eligible to drive that class of vehicle under this section.

Section 19–Disqualification or Revocation of Driving Licence

(1) If a licensing authority is satisfied, after giving the holder of a driving licence an opportunity of being heard, that he: (a) is a habitual criminal or a habitual drunkard; or (b) is a habitual addict to any narcotic drug or psychotropic substance within the meaning of the Narcotic Drugs and Psychotropic Substances Act, 1985; or (c) is using or has used a motor vehicle in the commission of a cognizable offence; or (d) has by his previous conduct as driver of a motor vehicle shown that his driving is likely to be attended with danger to the public; or (e) has obtained any driving licence or a licence to drive a particular class or description of motor vehicle by fraud

or misrepresentation; or (f) has committed any such act which is likely to cause nuisance or danger to the public, as may be prescribed by the Central Government, having regard to the objects of this Act; or (g) has failed to submit to, or has not passed, the tests referred to in the proviso to sub-section (3) of Section 22; or (h) being a person under the age of eighteen years who has been granted a learner's licence or a driving licence with the consent in writing of the person having the care of the holder of the licence and has ceased to be in such care, it may, for reasons to be recorded in writing, make an order, (i) disqualifying that person for a specified period for holding or obtaining any driving licence to drive all or any classes or descriptions of vehicles specified in the licence; or (ii) revoke any such licence.

(2) Where an order under sub-section (1) is made, the holder of a driving licence shall forthwith surrender his driving licence to the licensing authority making the order, if the driving licence has not already been surrendered, and the licensing authority shall: (a) if the driving licence is a driving licence issued under this Act, keep it until the disqualification has expired or has been removed; or (b) if it is not a driving licence issued under this Act, endorse the disqualification upon it and send it to the licensing authority by which it was issued; or (c) in the case of revocation of any licence, endorse the revocation upon it and if it is not the authority which issued the same, intimate the fact of revocation to the authority which issued that licence; provided that where the driving licence of a person authorises him to drive more than one class or description of motor vehicles and the order, made under sub-section (1), disqualifies him from driving any specified class or description of motor vehicles, the licensing authority shall endorse the disqualification upon the driving licence and return the same to the holder.

(3) Any person aggrieved by an order made by a licensing authority under sub-section (1) may, within thirty days of the receipt of the order, appeal to the prescribed authority, and

such appellate authority shall give notice to the licensing authority and hear either party if so required by that party and may pass such order as it thinks fit and an order passed by any such appellate authority shall be final.

Section 21–Suspension of Driving Licence in Certain Cases: (1) Where, in relation to a person who had been previously convicted of an offence punishable under Section 184, a case is registered by a police officer on the allegation that such person has, by such dangerous driving as is referred to in the said Section 184, of any class or description of motor vehicle caused the death of, or grievous hurt to, one or more persons, the driving licence held by such person shall in relation to such class or description of motor vehicle becomes suspended: (a) for a period of six months from the date on which the case is registered, or (b) if such person is discharged or acquitted before the expiry of the period aforesaid, until such discharge or acquittal, as the case may be.

Section 41(7)–Validity of Certificate of Registration: A certificate of registration issued under sub-section (3), whether before or after the commencement of this Act, in respect of a motor vehicle, other than a transport vehicle, shall, subject to the provisions contained in this Act, be valid only for a period of fifteen years from the date of issue of such certificate and shall be renewable.

Section 42–Special Provisions for Registration of Motor Vehicles of Diplomatic Officers: (1) Where an application for registration of a motor vehicle is made under sub-section (1) of Section 41 by or on behalf of any diplomatic officer or consular officer, then, notwithstanding anything contained in sub-section (3) or sub-section (6) of that section, the registering authority shall register the vehicle in such manner and in accordance with such procedure as may be provided by rules made in this behalf by the Central Government under sub-section (3) and shall assign to the vehicle for display thereon a special registration mark in accordance with the provisions contained in those rules and shall issue a certificate (hereafter in this section referred to as the certificate of registration) that the vehicle has been registered under this section; and any vehicle so registered shall not, so long as it remains the property of any diplomatic officer or consular officer, require to be registered otherwise under this Act.

Section 50–Transfer of Ownership: Where the ownership of any motor vehicle is transferred: (a) the transferor shall, (i) in the case of a vehicle registered within the same State, within fourteen days of the transfer, report the fact of transfer, in such form with such documents and in such manner, as may be prescribed by the Central Government to the registering authority within whose jurisdiction the transfer is to be effected and shall simultaneously send a copy of the said report to the transferee; and (ii) in the case of a vehicle registered outside the State, within forty-five days of the transfer, forward to the registering authority referred to in sub-clause (i), the no objection certificate obtained under Section 48.

Section 53–Suspension of Registration: (1) If any registering authority or other prescribed authority has reason to believe that any motor vehicle within its jurisdiction: (a) is in such a condition that its use in a public place would constitute a danger to the public, or that it fails to comply with the requirements of this Act or of the rules made thereunder, or (b) has been, or is being, used for hire or reward without a valid permit for being used as such, the authority may, after giving the owner an opportunity of making any representation he may wish to make (by sending to the owner a notice by registered post acknowledgment due at his address entered in the certificate of registration), for reasons to be recorded in writing, suspend the certificate of registration of the vehicle: (i) in any case falling under clause (a), until the defects are rectified to its satisfaction; and (ii) in any case falling under clause (b), for a period not exceeding 4 months.

Section 55–Cancellation of Registration: (1) If a motor vehicle has been destroyed or has been rendered permanently incapable of use, the owner shall, within fourteen days or as soon as may be, report the fact to the registering authority within whose jurisdiction he has the residence or place of business where the vehicle is normally kept, as the case may be, and shall forward to the authority the certificate of registration of the vehicle. (2) The registering authority shall, if it is the original registering authority, cancel the registration and the certificate of registration, or, if it is not, shall forward the report and the certificate of registration to the original registering authority and that authority shall cancel the registration.

Section 140–Liability to Pay Compensation in Certain Cases on the Principle of No Fault: (1) Where death or permanent disablement of any person has resulted from an accident arising out of the use of a motor vehicle or motor vehicles, the owner of the vehicle shall, or, as the case may be, the owners of the vehicles shall, jointly and severally, be liable to pay compensation in respect of such death or disablement in accordance with the provisions of this section.

(2) The amount of compensation which shall be payable under sub-section (1) in respect of the death of any person shall be fixed sum of fifty thousand rupees and the amount of compensation payable under that sub-section in respect of the permanent disablement of any person shall be a fixed sum of twenty five thousand rupees.

(3) In any claim for compensation under sub-section (1), the claimant shall not be required to plead and establish that the death or permanent disablement in respect of which the claim has been made was due to any wrongful act, neglect or default of the owner or owners of the vehicle or vehicles concerned or of any other person.

(4) A claim for compensation under sub-section (1) shall not be detected by reason of any wrongful act, neglect or default of the person in respect of whose death or permanent disablement the claim has been made nor shall the quantum of

compensation recoverable in respect of such death or permanent disablement be reduced on the basis of the share of such person in the responsibility for such death or permanent disablement.

Section 147–Requirements of Policies and Limits of Liability: (1) In order to comply with the requirements of this Chapter, a policy of insurance must be a policy which: (a) is issued by a person who is an authorised insurer; or (b) insurer the person or classes of persons specified in the policy to the extent specified in sub-section (2)(i) against any liability which may be incurred by him in respect of the death of or bodily injury to any person, [including owner of the goods or his authorised representative carried in the vehicle] or damage to any property of a third party caused by or arising out of the use of the vehicle in a public place; (ii) against the death of or bodily injury to any passenger of a public service vehicle caused by or arising out of the use of the vehicle in a public place. Provided that a policy shall not be required, (i) to cover liability in respect of the death, arising out of and in the course of his employment, of the employee of a person insured by the policy or in respect of bodily injury sustained by such an employee arising out of and in the course of his employment other than a liability arising under the Workmen's Compensation Act, 1923 (8 of 1923) in respect of the death of, or bodily injury to, any such employee: (a) engaged in driving the vehicle, or (b) if it is a public service vehicle engaged as conductor of the vehicle or in examining tickets on the vehicle, or (c) if it is a goods carriage, being carried in the vehicle, or (ii) to cover any contractual liability.

***Explanation*:** For the removal of doubts, it is hereby declared that the death of or bodily injury to any person or damage to any property of a third party shall be deemed to have been caused by or to have arisen out of, the use of a vehicle in a public place notwithstanding that the person who is dead or injured or the property which is damaged was not in a public place at the time of the accident, if the act or omission which led to the accident occurred in a public place.

(2) Subject to the proviso to sub-section (1), a policy of insurance referred to in sub-section (1), shall cover any liability incurred in respect of any accident, up to the following limits, namely: (a) save as provided in clause (b), the amount of liability incurred; and (b) in respect of damage to any property of a third party, a limit of rupees six thousand:

"Provided that any policy of insurance issued with any limited liability and in force, immediately before the commencement of this Act, shall continue to be effective for a period of four months after such commencement or till the date of expiry of such policy whichever is earlier".

(3) A policy shall be of no effect for the purposes of this Chapter unless and until there is issued by the insurer in favour of the person by whom the policy is effected a certificate of insurance in the prescribed form and containing the prescribed particulars of any condition subject to which the policy is issued and of any other prescribed matters; and different forms, particulars and matters may be prescribed in different cases.

(4) Where a cover note issued by the insurer under the provisions of this Chapter or the rules made there under is not followed by a policy of insurance within the prescribed time, the insurer shall, within seven days of the expiry of the period of the validity of the cover note, notify the fact to the registering authority in whose records the vehicle to which the cover note relates has been registered or to such other authority as the State Government may prescribe.

(5) Notwithstanding anything contained in any law for the time being in force, an insurer issuing a policy of insurance under this section shall be liable to indemnify the person or classes of persons specified in the policy in respect of any liability which the policy purports to cover in the case of that person or those classes of persons.

Section 148–Validity of Policies of Insurance Issued in Reciprocating Countries: Where, in pursuance of an arrangement between India and any reciprocating country, the motor vehicle registered in the reciprocating country operates on any route or within any area common to the two countries and there is in force in relation to the use of the vehicle in the reciprocating country, a policy of insurance complying with the requirements of the law of insurance in force in that country, then, notwithstanding anything contained in Section 147 but subject to any rules which may be made under Section 164, such policy of insurance shall be effective throughout the route or area in respect of which, the arrangement has been made, as if the policy of insurance had complied with the requirements of this Chapter.

Section 157–Transfer of Certificate of Insurance: (1) Where a person in whose favour the certificate of insurance has been issued in accordance with the provisions of this Chapter transfers to another person the ownership of the motor vehicle in respect of which such insurance was taken together with the policy of insurance relating thereto, the certificate of insurance and the policy described in the certificate shall be deemed to have been transferred in favour of the person to whom the motor vehicle is transferred with effect from the date of its transfer.

***Explanation*:** For the removal of doubts, it is hereby declared that such deemed transfer shall include transfer of rights and liabilities of the said certificate of insurance and policy of insurance.

(2) The transferee shall apply within fourteen days from the date of transfer in the prescribed form to the insurer for making necessary changes in regard to the fact of transfer in the certificate of insurance and the policy described in the certificate in his favour and the insurer shall make the necessary changes in the certificate and the policy of insurance in regard to the transfer of insurance.

Section 163–Scheme for Payment of Compensation in Case of Hit and Run Motor Accidents: (1) The Central Government may, by notification in the Official Gazette, make a scheme specifying, the manner in which the scheme shall be administered by the General Insurance Corporation, the form, manner and the time within which applications for compensation may be made, the officers or authorities to whom such applications may be made, the procedure to be followed by such officers or authorities for considering and passing orders on such applications, and all other matters connected with, or incidental to, the administration of the scheme and the payment of compensation.

(2) A scheme made under sub-section (1) may provide that: (a) a contravention of any provision thereof shall be punishable with imprisonment for such term as may be specified but in no case exceeding three months, or with fine which may extend to such amount as may be specified but in no case exceeding five hundred rupees or with both; (b) the powers, functions or duties conferred or imposed on any officer or authority by such scheme as may be delegated with the prior approval in writing of the Central Government, by such officer or authority to any other officer or authority; (c) any provision of such scheme that may operate with retrospective effect from a date not earlier than the date of establishment of the Solatium Fund under the Motor Vehicles Act, 1939 (4 of 1939) as it stood immediately before the commencement of this Act, "Provided that no such retrospective effect shall be given so as to prejudicially affect the interests of any person who may be governed by such provision".

Section 168–Award of the Claims Tribunal: (1) On receipt of an application for compensation made under Section 166, the claims tribunal shall, after giving notice of the application to the insurer and after giving the parties (including the insurer) an opportunity of being heard, hold an inquiry into the claim or, as the case may be, each of the claims and, subject to the provisions of Section 162 may make an award determining the amount of compensation which appears to it to be just and specifying the person or persons to whom compensation shall be paid and in making the award the claims tribunal shall specify the amount which shall be paid by the insurer or owner or driver of the vehicle involved in the accident or by all or any of them, as the case may be: Provided that where such application makes a claim for compensation under Section 140 in respect of the death or permanent disablement of any person, such claim and any other claim (whether made in such application or otherwise) for compensation in respect of such death or permanent disablement shall be disposed of in accordance with the provisions of Chapter X.

(2) The claims tribunal shall arrange to deliver copies of the award to the parties concerned expeditiously and in any case within a period of fifteen days from the date of the award.

(3) When an award is made under this section, the person who is required to pay any amount in terms of such award shall, within thirty days of the date of announcing the award by the claims tribunal, deposit the entire amount awarded in such manner as the claims tribunal may direct.

Section 184–Driving Dangerously: Whoever drives a motor vehicle at a speed or in a manner which is dangerous to the public, having regard to all the circumstances of the case including the nature, condition and use of the place where the vehicle is driven and the amount of traffic which actually is at the time or which might reasonably be expected to be in the place, shall be punishable for the first offence with imprisonment for a term which may extend to six months or with fine which may extend to one thousand rupees, and for any second or subsequent offence, if committed within three years of the commission of a previous similar offence with imprisonment for a term which may extend to two years or with fine which may extend to two thousand rupees, or with both.

Types of Claims

Any accident involving a motor vehicle may give rise to

two types of claims viz., own damage claims because of damages to the vehicle and third party claims because of death or bodily injuries to third parties or property damage of property belonging to third party. While own damage claims are settled by the companies, the third party claims are reported before Motor Accident Claims Tribunals for adjudication. The procedure of settlement of both types of claims is given below.

Own Damage Claims: On happening of any claim involving damages to motor vehicle, immediate notice be given to the insurance company along with a copy of the insurance policy, copy of driving licence and estimated cost of repairs. In case the accident has occurred in a city other than the one where policy was issued, the notice may be given to the nearest office of the insurance company. On receipt of notice of claim, the insurance company checks the policy to see whether it is the same vehicle which is insured, whether the policy is valid on the date of accident and whether the vehicle is comprehensively insured. The claim is registered and the insured is given claim form in which details regarding the vehicle, policy, driver, cause of accident, place where vehicle is lying for inspection, any third party loss etc. are asked. The insured is asked to return the same duly filled in along with estimate of repairs and thereafter the surveyor is appointed to assess the loss. The surveyor examines the vehicle minutely to inspect the damages and to decide which part is repairable and which needs replacement. He authorises the repairer to replace the damaged parts and also finalises the repair charges with the repairer. Thereafter, he submits his report to the insurance company and the insured is required to submit bills of parts and repairs and also deposit the salvage of damaged parts. The report is examined at the office of insurance company and bills are checked up. After finding the bills in order, the assessed amount is paid to the insured.

Third Party Claims: As explained under the provisions of MV Act, special Motor Accident Claims Tribunals

(MACTs) have been set up under Section 165 of MV Act and the civil courts are barred to adjudicate the matters of granting compensation to the victims of motor vehicle accidents.

The victim of a motor vehicle accident or his legal heirs (in case of death) files petition before MACT u/s 140 as well as 166 of the MV Act impleading the driver, owner and insurer of the offending vehicle as respondents.

The procedure of awarding interim compensation also known as no fault liability has been explained in the preceding paras while discussing provisions of the Motor Vehicle Act. The insurance company gets the matter investigated through their panel investigators to gather the following information:

1. Policy of vehicle.
2. Driver at the time of accident and details of his driving licence.
3. Validity of the driving licence on the date of accident and for the class of vehicle.
4. Whether the driver was under the influence of liquor or intoxicating drugs.
5. Purpose for which the vehicle was being used at the time of accident.
6. Whether any other person or vehicle is also responsible for causing the accident.
7. Details about the age, salary, legal heirs of the deceased.
8. Whether there was any violation of any policy condition etc.

In case there is any violation of policy condition and a defence is available under Section 149(2) of the MV Act, or the case is defended and proper evidence is led, the income and age of deceased and the dependency has to be proved by the claimants.

After hearing the arguments, the MACT passes the award and the insurer may satisfy the same by making the payment in terms of the award or file appeal u/s 173 MV Act in case any ground is available and the award is found to be perverse.

Lok Adalats

If case liability of the insurer is admitted and there is no violation of any policy conditions, such claims could be placed before lok adalats for settlement. The concept of lok adalats is a novel concept and is beneficial for all the parties. The claimants get the money at a time when it is needed most. The insurers save on interest and it brings an end to litigation as no appeal can be filed in cases settled before the lok adalats. The judiciary's disposal rate is increased and backlog is cleared.

Therefore, efforts should be made to place maximum cases before lok adalats and get these settled to bring back smiles on the faces of victims of road accidents and/or their legal heirs.

Annexure 9

Fatal Accidents Act, 1855

An Act to provide compensation to families for loss occasioned by the death of a person caused by actionable wrong.

Preamble

Whereas no action or suit is now maintainable in any court against a person who, by his wrongful act, neglect or default, may have caused the death of another person, and it is often times right and expedient that the wrongdoer in such case should be answerable in damages for the injury so caused by him.

1. Short Title and Extent:

(1) This Act may be called the Fatal Accidents Act, 1855.

(2) It extends to the whole of India except the State of Jammu and Kashmir.

1A. Suit for Compensation to the Family of a Person for Loss Occasioned to it by His Death by Actionable Wrong

Whenever the death of a person shall be caused by wrongful act, neglect, or default, and the act, neglect or default is such as would (if death had not ensured) have entitled the party injured to maintain an action and recover damages in respect thereof, the party who would have been liable if death had not ensured, shall be liable to an action or suit for damages, notwithstanding the death of the person injured, and although the death shall have been caused under such circumstances as amount in law to felony or other crime.

Every such action or suit shall be for the benefit of the wife, husband, parent and child, if any, of the person whose death shall have been so caused, and shall be brought by and in the name of the executor, administrator, or representative of the person deceased; and in every such action, the court may give such damages as it may think proportioned to the loss resulting from such death to the parties respectively, for whom and for whose benefit such action shall be brought, and the amount so recovered, after deducting all costs and expenses, including the costs not recovered from the defendant, shall be divided amongst the before-mentioned parties, or any of them, in such shares as the court by its judgement or decree shall direct.

2. Not More Than One Suit to be Brought

Provided always that not more than one action or suit shall be brought for, and in respect of, the same subject matter of complaint.

Claim for loss to the estate may be added. Provided that in any such action or suit, the executor, administrator, or representative of the deceased may insert a claim for, and recover any pecuniary loss, to the estate of the deceased occasioned by such wrongful act, neglect or default, which sum, when recovered, shall be deemed part of the assets of the estate of the deceased.

3. Plaintiff Shall Deliver Particulars Etc.

The plaint in any such action or suit shall give a full particular of the person or persons for whom, or on whose behalf, such action or suit shall be brought, and of the nature of the claim in respect of such damages shall be sought to be recovered.

4. Interpretation Clause

The following words and expressions are intended to have the meanings hereby assigned to them respectively, so far as such meanings are not excluded by the context or by the nature of the subject-matter; that is to say, the word "person" shall apply to bodies politic and corporate; and the word "parent" shall include father and mother, grandfather and grandmother; and the word "child" shall include son and daughter, and grandson and granddaughter, and stepson and stepdaughter.

Annexure 10

Workmen's Compensation Act, 1923

The Workmen's Compensation Act, 1923 provides for payment of compensation to workmen and their dependants in case of injury and accident (including certain occupational diseases) arising out of and in the course of employment and resulting in disablement or death. The Act applies to railway servants and persons employed in any such capacity as is specified in Schedule II of the Act. The Schedule II includes persons employed in factories, mines, plantations, mechanically propelled vehicles, construction works and certain other hazardous occupations.

The Act also specifies a list of diseases, which, if contracted by the worker, would be deemed to be an occupational disease peculiar to that employment which shall be deemed to be an injury by accident liable for compensation under the Act.

Workman means any person (other than a person whose employment is of a casual nature and who is employed for purposes other than of the employer's trade or business) as specified in the Act and its Schedule. However, the Central Government or the State Government may add to the Schedule any class of persons employed in any occupation which is a hazardous occupation.

The amount of compensation to be paid depends on the nature of the injury and the average monthly wages and age of workmen. The minimum and maximum rates of compensation payable for death (in such cases it is paid to the dependents of workmen) and for disability have been fixed and is subject to revision from time to time.

A Social Security Division has been set up under the Ministry of Labour and Employment, Government of India which deals with framing of social security policy for the workers and implementation of the various social security schemes. It is also responsible for enforcing this Act. The Act is administered by the State Governments through commissioners for Workmen's Compensation.

The main provisions of the Act are as under:

1. An employer is liable to pay compensation: (i) if personal injury is caused to a workman by accident arising out of and in the course of his employment; and (ii) if a workman employed in any employment contracts any disease, specified in the Act as an occupational disease peculiar to that employment.
2. However, the employer is not liable to pay compensation in the following cases:

- If the injury does not result in the total or partial disablement of the workman for a period exceeding three days.
- If the injury, not resulting in death or permanent total disablement, is caused by an accident which is directly attributable to: (i) the workman having been at the time of the accident under the influence of drink or drugs; or (ii) the willful disobedience of the workman to an order expressly given, or to a rule expressly framed, for the purpose of securing the safety of workmen; or (iii) the willful removal or disregard by the workman of any safety guard or other device which has been provided for the purpose of securing safety of workmen.

3. The State Government may, by notification in the Official Gazette, appoint any person to be a commissioner for Workmen's Compensation for such area as may be specified in the notification. Any commissioner may, for the purpose of deciding any matter referred to him for decision under this Act, choose one or more persons possessing special knowledge of any matter relevant to the matter under inquiry to assist him in holding the inquiry.

4. Compensation shall be paid as soon as it falls due. In cases where the employer does not accept the liability for compensation to the extent claimed, he shall be bound to make provisional payment based on the extent of liability which he accepts, and, such payment shall be deposited with the commissioner or made to the workman, as the case may be.
5. If any question arises in any proceedings under this Act as to the liability of any person to pay compensation (including any question as to whether a person injured is or is not a workman) or as to the amount or duration of compensation (including any question as to the nature or extent of disablement), the question shall, in default of agreement, be settled by a commissioner. No civil court shall have jurisdiction to settle, decide or deal with any question which is by or under this Act required to be settled, decided or dealt with by a commissioner or to enforce any liability incurred under this Act.
6. The State Government may, by notification in the Official Gazette, direct that every person employing workmen, or that any specified class of such persons, shall send at such time and in such form and to such authority, as may be specified in the notification, a correct return specifying the number of injuries in respect of which compensation has been paid by the employer during the previous year and the amount of such compensation together with such other particulars as to the compensation as the State Government may direct.
7. Whoever, fails to maintain a notice book which he is required to maintain; or fails to send to the commissioner a statement which he is required to send; or fails to send a report which he is required to send; or fails to make a return which he is required to make, shall be punishable with fine.

Annexure 11

A Brief Case Analysis: Bhopal Gas Leak Disaster

Union Carbide Corporation vs. Union of India, AIR, 1992 SC 248

Authorities:

Constitution of India: Articles 48A and 51A
Indian Penal Code, 1860: Section 304A; Sections 336, 337 and 338 read with Section 35
Acts: Public Liability Insurance Act, 1991
Bhopal Gas Leak Disaster (Processing of Claims) Act, 1985
Scheme: Bhopal Gas Leak Disaster (Registration and Processing of Claims) Scheme, 1985
Tort Cases: *M.C. Mehta vs. Union of India* (Oleum Gas Leak Case, 1985)
Rylands vs. Fletcher
Bano vs. Union Carbide
Sahu vs. Union Carbide
Texas City Refinery Case
Caparo vs. Dickman
United States vs. Carroll

Introduction

It was the night of December 23, 1984, when one of the worst disasters of its time took place in Bhopal, the capital city of Madhya Pradesh in India. It was caused by the leakage of Methyl Isocyanate (MIC) and other toxic gases from the plant of Union Carbide India Ltd. (UICL), which manufactures pesticides etc. in Bhopal. UICL happens to be a subsidiary of US multinational Union Carbide Corporation (UCC).

The mass disaster took a heavy toll causing the death of not less than 3,000 persons and left serious injuries to over six lakh people, permanently affecting their eyes, respiratory system, and causing scores of other complications resulting in permanent disability and even damaging the foetus of pregnant women.

Since most of the victims belonged to the lower economic strata, the claim of compensation involving such a large number of victims posed a peculiar problem. The case matter relates to law of tort as such regards the loss spread, moral and social hazard and transaction cost. The case analysis focuses mainly on the importance of law with respect to economic perspective as well as social justice perspective.

A large number of cases were filed on behalf of victims both in Bhopal as well as in US against the UCC. An effort by the Government of India and the UCC for out of court settlement resulted in a failure. Global welfare groups like "Greenpeace" raised the issue to ensure proper compensation for the victims and to create effective system so that such incident may not be repeated in future.

Facts

1. The Government of India became the sole representative of the victims in any case of compensation against UCIL by enacting Bhopal Gas Leak Disaster (Processing of Claims) Act, 1985.
2. It filed a suit against the UCC in the United States District Court of New York claiming US dollars 3.3 billion.
3. The US Court denied the Indian stand and dismissed the suit on the grounds *of forum non conveniens,* i.e., suit can be more conveniently tried in India.
4. The Union of India filed a suit in the District Court of Bhopal. The District and Sessions Judge ordered the UCC to pay an interim relief of ₹ 350 crore to the gas victims.
5. In an appeal, the Madhya Pradesh High Court reduced the quantum of ₹ 350 crore to ₹ 250 crore.
6. The UCC tried a direct settlement with the gas victims but the District and Sessions Judge directed UCC not to make

any settlement or compromise with any individual until further orders.

7. The UCC also tried to negotiate with the Union of India for an out of court settlement.
8. Throughout 1990, the Indian Supreme Court heard appeals against the settlement from "activist petitions".
9. In 1991, the Supreme Court upheld the compensation of US$470 million and ordered that any other outstanding petitions that challenge the original decision stand to be dismissed.
10. It also requested UCC to fund a hospital to treat the victims of the disaster.

Issues

1. Did the Indian Government took precautions in terms of laying down strict regulations for a factory of such nature?
2. Had proper care been taken by UCIL under the law?
3. Had the individuals got the resources to file case against UCC in the United States?
4. Had the United States used its developed mechanism of the law of torts in providing fair trial?
5. Was the Indian judicial system empowered and equipped to handle cases of such magnitude?
6. Was the damage measured on a scale of fair compensation?
7. Should there be universal jurisdiction in the case of law of torts?

Rules Applicable

The first and foremost form of tort laws is negligence, which is applicable in this case. Negligence is a failure to exercise due care which is proved by the injured person who can recover damages to compensate for their harm to bare body, property, mental being and financial status.

The proceedings were initiated under Section 304A, and Sections 336, 337, and 338 read with Section 35 of the Indian

Penal Code, 1860. Section 304A deals with death by negligence. Sections 336, 337 and 338 deal with the offences of endangering life and personal safety of others. This is read along with Section 35 which deals with the aspect of common intention.

As far as the legal position of the case is concerned in *M.C. Mehta vs. Union of India*, the Supreme Court laid down the rule of "absolute liability" in preference to the rule of strict liability as laid down in *Ryland vs. Fletcher*.

The principle of absolute liability states that when an enterprise is engaged in hazardous or inherently dangerous industry such as if harm results due to such activity, the enterprise is strictly liable to compensate all those and would have no excuse that it had taken due care and there is no negligence on its part. The concept of absolute liability in India grew stronger due to the impetus given by Bhopal Gas Disaster and the Oleum Gas leak case.

In order to provide the victims due to the handling of hazardous substance, an expeditious relief, the Government passed the Public Liability Insurance Act, 1991. In 1976, through amendment, Articles 48A and 51A were inserted in the Constitution of India. Through this, the state as well as the citizens, were constitutionally obliged to protect and conserve the natural resources.

Judgement

Keeping in consideration all the facts and the urgency of the case, the Supreme Court on April 30, 1993, gave a direction that the settlement amount to US$ 470 million and interest thereby from it, should be utilized only for the payment of compensation to about 6 lakh victims and under no circumstances it should be utilized for payment of interim relief. All related cases shall stand transferred and concluded in terms of settlement and all criminal proceedings arising out of the disaster shall stand quashed wherever these may be pending.

Analysis

The enormity of the case puts two aspects together for consideration, the perspective of law and the perspective of economics. The impact of tort law and the impact of tort damages—deterrence, ensuring justice, fairness and distribution are the prime concerns. Determination of responsibility and the extent of compensation are the other factors.

As per the investigation, the Government as well as the UCIL fell short of safety measures, hence a clear suggestion of negligence was witnessed. US Government shielded UCC and the Indian Government pursued the matter in a disappointing way, resulting in the mockery of justice for the victims. Indian tort law showed its immaturity and compensation awarded was not enough, seeing the massiveness of damage. Indian judiciary came with a rather strict principle, "The Doctrine of Absolute Liability" to ensure maintenance of standards for public safeguard at large. A proper tort law, whereby the public gets the power to sue the erring company was seen as one of the solutions.

Guideline cases included:

Caparo vs. Dickman (1990): To establish duty of care, harm must be: (a) reasonably foreseeable; (b) proximity between the plaintiff and defendant; (c) it has to be fair, just and reasonable. *Perre vs. Apand* (1999) upheld this principle. *United States vs. Carroll Towing Co.* (1947) determined the standard of care for the tort of negligence. *M.C. Mehta vs. The Union of India*, Oleum gas leak case (1985) determined the absolute liability of all those who are affected without any exception. In *Rylands vs. Fletcher*, it was viewed that the compensation must have a deterrent effect. The Texas City Refinery case (2005) had similar issues as of the Bhopal case. Personal injury cases were also heard and the compensation was awarded which showed a well developed torts law and awareness towards it.

Conclusion

The administrative system and the judicial system failed miserably in handling such a massive devastation against humanity. Substantial relief, rehabilitation, proper medical facilities and compensation have still been an illusion. Duty and obligation of state as a welfare state must be established.

References

Websites

http://www.academia.edu.com.

http://www.s3amazonaws.com.

http://en.wikipedia.org/wiki/Bhopal_disaster.

http://www.greenpeace.org/usa/en/campaigns/toxics/justice-for-Bhopal.

http://www.indiankanoon.org/docfragment/654007/?forminput=union%20carbide%20corporation.

http://www.hindustantimes.com/india-news/bhopal/panel-visits-bmhrc-in-bhopal-not-happy-with-facilities/article1-1257770.aspx.

http://www.preservearticles.com/201101143273/case-study-of-bhopal-gas-leak-disaster.html.

Books

- Butterworth's Common Law Series (The Law of Damage, Tort, Negligence and Contract), Lexis Nexis.
- Lexis Nexis Quick Reference Guide: Law of Torts.

Annexure 12

Law of Torts

Syllabus for University Examination and Recommended Readings

Syllabus

1. Nature and definition of tort.
2. Tort distinguished from crime and contract.
3. General differences in tort: *Volenti non fit injuria*, act of God, inevitable accident, statutory authority.
4. Vicarious liability: Master's liability for act of servant.
5. Remoteness of damage.
6. Absolute and strict liability.
7. Tort against person: Assault, battery, false imprisonment.
8. Tort against property: Nuisance.
9. Tort of negligence: Essentials, contributory negligence, rule of *res ipra loguitur*.
10. Consumer Protection Act, 1986: Salient features, consumer dispute redressal agencies.
11. Salient features of the Motor Vehicle Act, 1988 with special reference to compulsory insurance: Insurer's liability for third party risks.

Recommended Readings

1. Agrawala's, *Pleadings and Precedents in India.*
2. Arun Kumar, *Law of Torts.*
3. Ashok K. Jain, *Law of Torts.*
4. G.K. Puri, *Law of Torts.*
5. R. Chandra, *Law of Torts.*
6. R.K. Bangia, *Law of Torts.*

7. Ratanlal and Dhirajlal, *Law of Torts.*
8. Salmond and Hueston, *Law of Torts.*
9. Universal Publishers, *Law of Torts.*
10. W.V.H. Rogers, *Law of Torts*.
11. Winfield and Jolowicz, *On Torts.*

Index

Index